Everyone's talking about
# Lea DeLaria

She's the straight-talking comic most likely to exceed. Her critically acclaimed one-woman show, *It's Delightful, It's Delicious, It's DeLaria,* has played to sold-out houses in major venues across the country. And her show-stopping performances have wowed both crowds and critics alike. From Hollywood to Broadway, people just can't stop raving about Lea DeLaria. . . .

"A STAR IS BORN WITH LEA DELARIA."
—*Entertainment Weekly*

"A PHENOMENON."
—*Los Angeles Times*

"EVERY INCH A STAR."
—*The New York Times*

And that's just the beginning . . .
## Lea's Book of Rules for the World

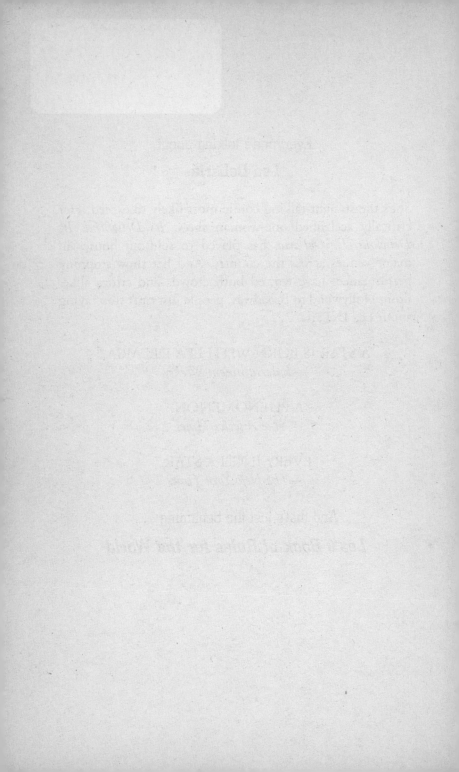

# Lea DeLaria

with Maggie Cassella

## LEA'S BOOK OF RULES

## FOR THE WORLD

A DELL TRADE PAPERBACK

A DELL TRADE PAPERBACK

Published by
Dell Publishing
a division of
Random House, Inc.
1540 Broadway
New York, New York 10036

Cover photos by Lynn Goldsmith

Dell books may be purchased for business or promotional use or for special sales. For information please write to: Special Markets Department, Random House, Inc., 1540 Broadway, New York, N.Y. 10036.

DTP and the colophon are trademarks of Random House, Inc.

Designed by Jessica Shatan

Library of Congress Cataloging in Publication Data

DeLaria, Lea.
  Lea's book of rules for the world / by Lea DeLaria with Maggie Cassella.
    p. cm.
  ISBN 0-440-50854-1
  1. DeLaria, Lea.  2. Comedians—United States—Biography.  3. Actors—United States—Biography.  4. American wit and humor.  I. Cassella, Maggie.  II. Title.
PN2287.D365 A3  2000
792.7′028′092—dc21
[B]
99-054302

Printed in the United States of America

Published simultaneously in Canada

May 2000

10 9 8 7 6 5 4 3 2 1

FFG

*For J.D. and her little "p"*

# ACKNOWLEDGMENTS

This book would have been an impossibility without the love and support of the two individuals who have helped me make a life filled with riches, Vladimir the Impaler and Al Roker. I am a better person for having known them.

*Special Thanks to:*
Maggie Cassella, Terry dANUSer, Tom Spain, Jesse Tyler Furgeson, George Wolfe, Shannon Burkett, Scott Thompson, Paul Rudnick, Sandra Bernhard, Jeremy Katz, Mel Burger, David Kolodner, Mark Swartz, my beautiful family, the entire city of Portland, OR, and any woman with whom I've made the beast with two backs.

# CONTENTS

Dear Editor,
Your March cover shot of Lea DeLaria was missing one thing—an apple in her mouth. As Gertrude Stein would put it, "A pig is a pig is a pig." What comes out of De-Laria's mouth should be rerouted to its proper place—a white bowl that you can flush. She is a disgrace to the gay and lesbian community, except to those whose sense of humor is restricted to what a bird does on the head of a statue.

Tom Gibbons
Los Angeles

Dear Editor,
The first reaction I experienced upon witnessing Lea De-Laria's portly figure tainting the cover of your respectable publication was that of a gag reflex. As an Italian-American lesbian, I must say that DeLaria is *not* an asset to the gay community. DeLaria can bad-mouth Ellen De-Generes as much as she wants, but the fact is that I and, I'm sure, many other lesbians would rather be represented by Ellen any day of the week.

Heather Pighetti
Easthampton, Mass.

Dear Editor,
Some of the most demeaning things in my experience as a woman and a lesbian are men who treat women like objects, property, and pieces of meat. These men also call

women names, make obscene gestures, or worst of all, get their kicks from little girls. These men are insecure, crass individuals who obviously, when looking in the mirror, are not seeing what the rest of the world sees. Now imagine one of these men as a lesbian media darling. Crazy, right? Can you say Lea DeLaria? When are we going to stop giving this (woman?) so much press? The only thing I'm thankful for is we didn't get a repeat of the *Out* magazine cover. I'm still recovering from that!

Denise McCanles
West Hollywood, CA

Dear Editor,
I'd like to counter "Lea DeLaria's Top Pop Culture Picks" with one of my own: Lea DeLaria stranded on a desert island, all by herself, with no hope of rescue—or access to the media.

Michelle Mindlin
West Hollywood, CA

Dear Editor,
As the Executive Director of the Gay & Lesbian Alliance Against Defamation (GLAAD) I am writing to address Lea DeLaria's disparaging comments about GLAAD ("Lea DeLaria Goes Deep" May '98). Lea's language and crude remarks directed towards Chastity Bono, GLAAD Entertainment Media Director, and in turn, to the entire organization, were offensive and misleading.

Since 1985, GLAAD has worked with an unwavering dedication to ensure fair, accurate and inclusive representation in the media as a means of challenging discrimination based on sexual orientation and identity. With GLAAD offices based in six cities across the nation, we are constantly working with print journalists, news producers, television sit-com and drama producers and movie studios. GLAAD's response to homophobia is always prompt, decisive and issued with the hope of inviting dialogue that results in productive change.

Healthy difference, disagreement and debate are essential elements to the strength and survival of all communities. Particularly ours. Unfortunately, Lea's comments were not made in such a spirit.

Lea knows—firsthand—that GLAAD strives to foster a safe and accessible climate so that we all can pursue our personal and professional aspirations. Just last month, Lea accepted an invitation to perform on GLAAD's stage during our annual Media Awards.

The applause she received that night has faded. But her words have not.

Joan M. Garry, Executive Director
Gay & Lesbian Alliance Against Defamation

# INTRODUCTION

People find me offensive. Some people actually find me horribly offensive. These are the same people who think Bob Saget is talented. Still others go further. They put me on the Despicable Characters List.

### the despicable characters list

### 1. Slobodan Milosevic

### 2. Lea DeLaria

### 3. Kathie Lee Gifford

I'm entertaining at the Texas Lesbian Conference. As you can imagine, I am enthralled at the prospect of performing for any person who would actually choose to live in Texas, and certain that my observations will run closely to those who would opt for a weekend of fun at anything called a "Lesbian Conference."

I wait on the hotel ballroom-type, Tonka toy stage; "Tonka toy" because this is like all gay slash lesbian function slash shows in that most effort and expense is spent on the balloons. Forget that Lea is a fat chick on a rickety stage, buy the balloons. Never mind that the sound engineer is smoked-up, two hours behind schedule, and plans to use a Radio Shack microphone, because we got balloons! Don't try to fix the audible, drunken wedding reception next door, or the blown generator, or the bomb threat we just received from some constipated creepy Christians. No, just keep right on blowing up those lavender balloons. Sometimes, if I am really lucky, they have rainbow balloons.

So I stand there on that stage, that rickety Tonka toy stage, surrounded by those ever-present lavender balloons, listening to the wedding reception band singing "D-I-V-O-R-C-E," thinking, what an odd song to play at a wedding. I am supposed to be thinking about speaking. Right now I find it difficult, what with the band and the fact that my Radio Shack microphone is feeding back badly, although not badly enough to distract me from the blinking, coffee-can lighting, which is supposed to allow the audience to see me and is instead, I am certain, giving someone an epileptic fit. So I stand there.

I stand there looking out over a sea of lesbians with bad hairdos, when finally it all becomes too much and I snap. I notice the size of my audience. Allow me to clarify. I don't mean the size, as in number of members; I refer instead to the numbers of members of size. This isn't an audience. It's a herd.

Now, at some point in your life you have been in a situation like this. You look about a room and notice something awry. Let's say everyone is wearing a matching outfit, or perhaps they all have the same hat, or Down's syndrome. If you do notice, you are most likely to think some way or another about it. The main difference between you and me is this: If I think some way or another about anything, I will tell you.

"Is it a law in Texas that you have to weigh three hundred ninety-five pounds to be a lesbian?" I say.

The herd is silent. I continue.

"I mean, I'm a proud fat woman and all, but I think there's a slight problem when I'm the most svelte person in a room."

The herd blinks. I finish.

"You guys could eat a vegetable once in a while."

The herd boos. I get so booed. I am being booed by a herd of fat Texan lesbians sporting bad hairdos, some of whom have mustaches, all of whom reek of herbal tea.

They boo me because I have an opinion that differs from theirs.

In this, the new millennium, an individual is no longer permitted the luxury of expressing a unique thought. One must couch all ideas within the accepted garbage verbiage that makes up Political Correctness.

For example, Political Correctness advises that we avoid the use of perfume, as it has a trigger effect on the "environmentally impaired." What exactly is "environmentally impaired"? Is that when you can't distinguish whether or not you are outside? Can't we just say "allergic"? No, because then we are breaking P.C. Rule #1001:

## p.c. rule #1001

**Why say something**

**with one word**

**when you can use twenty?**

While appearing on *The Keenen Ivory Wayans Show*, Margaret Cho uses the words "dildo" and "penis." Penis is bleeped but dildo is allowed to travel the airways. Why censor one and not the other? How is a penis dirtier than a representation of a penis? Every man wears a penis. Every woman does not wear a dildo. Not even every lesbian wears a dildo. Of course, I do, and that, gentle reader, is why I'm the one writing the book.

People should be allowed to say what they think. It's just an idea; it doesn't have a life of its own. It's not going to pay taxes or go to college. It won't call you in the middle of dinner and try to sell you insurance. It will just hang there occupying space. As long as it doesn't hurt anybody—why not? It's basic, really. The trick is this: Don't allow it to matter, then it won't piss you off.

Take Camille Paglia, who has brought forth this concept: "Women are raped because of low self-esteem." As if I could awaken one morning, a few days before my period, look in a mirror, feel bloated and ugly, then *Bam*! I'm raped just like that and I still have the rest of my day.

You see, I obviously disagree with Ms. Paglia, but I do not find her offensive simply because we differ on the origin of rape. I don't find Camille offensive at all. In fact, I would fuck her if she were twenty-five years younger with a bag over her head. Of course, I'd also have to be drunk.

I have spent the majority of my life being told by parents, nuns, government officials, gas station jockies, meter maids, window washers, massage chicks who give full release, and Walter Mondale that I go too far. I push the envelope. I BREAK THE RULES.

Even the gay and lesbian community constantly complains about me. I have one question.

## lea's one question

### Is there such a thing as a gay and lesbian community?

Aren't we just a bunch of factioned-off individuals who do not trust each other? Yes. We yell at each other and scream at each other; in fact, if we spent half the time we spend hollering at each other hollering at the UNITED STATES GOVERNMENT we would have received our rights years ago. Then I could just relax on Gay Pride Day instead of marching behind a banner that reads THE OUT, PROUD LESBIGAY AND TRANSGENDERED RAINBOW DIVERSITY COALITION ON UNITY AND TOLERANCE.

Recently I received a commendation from Alan Hevesi, controller of the city of New York. I like Alan. They say he will run for mayor. I say anyone but Rudolph, except for maybe Bob Saget.

The commendation reads as follows:

### commendation presented to lea delaria

For her outstanding body of work as
an actress, singer, and comedian; for
her commitment to breaking ground
and opening minds as an openly gay
performer who communicates her
unique viewpoint on lesbian and
gay life; and for her dedication
to sharing both her tremendous
talents and her dynamic spirit
with audiences around the world.

I am presented this honor by Alan, who mentions my "incredible and critically acclaimed performance in *Our Town*." Alan meant *On the Town*, however, I cannot resist. "Thanks, Alan," I say as I receive my plaque. "It was a joy to play Emily."

Something happens to me that day. I should feel a sense of pride and accomplishment. The truth is I am bitter. Maybe it's Matthew Shepard, AIDS, the Holocaust, or the subway.

I begin to tell a story:

## my story

The day I was notified of this honor I went out. It was a Saturday night and I felt like having some fun. *The Most Fabulous Story Ever Told*, starring Lea DeLaria and Jesse Tyler Ferguson, had just closed. *On the Town*, starring Lea DeLaria and Jesse Tyler Ferguson, also closed . . . Jesse and I are pleased to announce that we are going into *Cats*. You only have to look at me once to know I have Mr. Mistoffolees written all over me.

As I mentioned, it was Saturday night, a night for fighting . . . traffic, that is, and I was once again ensconced in a New York City cab. We were clipping along Bleecker, when we found ourselves trapped behind a police car. The car was stopped dead in the middle of the street, so no one could pass. The officers inside had stopped in order to cruise the line of people waiting to get into Life, a hip urban trendy NYC night spot. They were cruising the line of people waiting to get into Life because it was filled with beautiful young women fashionably dressed in tight short skirts.

My meter was running. I was annoyed. The cabdriver

was leery of honking at a cop car, so we just sat there watching my money go out the window.

Finally the officers noticed the anxious lineup behind them and graciously moved over to allow us to pass. My meter read $29.53. I exaggerate slightly for effect.

I'm the type-o-gal who can't let things slide. I'm also the type-o-gal who buys those Voguelleish magazines containing the article "What Women Really Want." Once procured I hungrily read through looking for my name.

## <u>what women really want</u>

### 1. A good backrub

### 2. Financial independence

### 3. Lea DeLaria

### 4. World peace

As we drive by the thin blue line, I poke my head out.

"Hey, my meter's running, you know," I yell.

"I'm doing my job, you dyke bitch," the man who I pay to protect me from such violence screams back.

When I reach the "dyke bitch" part of my story there grows in the room a large intake of collective breath.

I pause to allow the gasp to wane, then look directly at Mr. Alan Hevesi, a New York City official.

"You know, Alan," I demure, "if I had known looking at pretty girls in tight short skirts was part of a policeman's job, I would have joined New York's Finest long ago."

Some people think that was going too far. *Breaking the rules*. I know Joan Garry does. You read the letter. She was responding to my telling Chastity Bono to "eat my dyke ass" in a *Lesbian News* cover story on me. I told Chastity to perform this particular task because Ms. *I Sprang from the Loins of Sonny and Cher* said in a *Los Angeles Times* article that "Ellen DeGeneres's show is too gay." Joan Garry, the executive director of GLAAD, seems in her letter to be upset with my "vulgarity." Didn't Lenny Bruce do this over thirty years ago? Words are meaningless symbols. It's the ideas behind the words that matter. Ergo my words to Chastity, "eat my dyke ass," are not remotely as vulgar as her openly homophobic words "Ellen DeGeneres's show is too gay." When you take into consideration Chastity's job as media spokesperson for GLAAD, an organization that is supposed to stop homophobic remarks in the media, then you must conclude Chastity Bono's words surpass vulgarity into nasty. Her words were nastier than rimming Tipper Gore.

Broke the rules again, didn't I? And speaking of breaking the rules, allow me to boldly go where no man dares to tread.

On May 3, 1999, I was snubbed by the Tony nominating committee. I had spent approximately two years working on *On the Town*. During this period I was told by everyone from Nathan Lane to Rosie O'Donnell that I would win the Tony. In fact, you can catch footage of me knocking wood, screaming at Rosie for jinxing me . . . little did we know, huh, Rosie?

I enjoyed doing Rosie's show. I enjoy it every time. On this particular show Rosie and I were supposed to do a duet. It did not happen. When I asked Rosie why, she replied, "Oh, Lea, I only sing with people who can't sing, like Helen Reddy." Lea, that's breaking the rules. . . .

## the 1999 tony nominations
## best performance by a featured actress in a musical

1. Kristin Chenoweth
*You're a Good Man, Charlie Brown*

2. Valarie Pettiford
*Fosse*

3. Mary Testa
*On the Town*

4. Gretha Boston
*It Ain't Nothin' But the Blues*

All of these women are good women. All are dynamic performers. All deserve their nominations. All I know is that when this list was read at 8:30 A.M. in Sardi's on May 3, 1999, the media and journalists and other interested theatergoers booed and hissed. Loudly.

I don't know why I was snubbed. I know I stopped the show eight times a week. I know George Wolfe called me to say two very important things:

## important things george wolfe said

1. You are bearing the weight of the responsibility of your artistry.

2. Einstein opined, "Great spirits have always encountered tremendous opposition from mediocre minds."

If George Wolfe had a vagina I'd marry him.

Who's George Wolfe, you say? For the Broadway impaired, George Wolfe is the artistic director of the Public

Theater. He helped create *Angels in America, Jelly's Last Jam*, and *Bring in Da Noise, Bring in Da Funk*, has won two Tony Awards for Best Director, and is considered by many to be a genius of modern American theater. That's his creative side. On a personal scale, George and I were split from the same DNA, which is difficult, considering his mother is a black educator, my mother is a white secretary, and we're of the opposite sex, although we are not entirely certain of the sex part.

Was using George's name and vagina in the same sentence breaking the rules? To quote great American musical theater, "You Bet Your Ass."*

Who wrote these uptight rules? What Puritan came over on the fucking *Mayflower* and said, "Here are *the rules*"? FUCK THE RULES.

I've been breaking the rules my whole life. Some say I've made a change, others a mess. On May 3, 1999, when my Tony snub was announced, I received a call from my father.

"Honey, do you think this happened because of your sexual orientation?"

My answer to my father's question I will keep between him and me, for that is our business. As for you, gentle reader, I will say one thing . . . my seventy-year-old Italian father used the words "sexual orientation" in a sentence.

Perhaps we need some new rules.

---

* For the nonfaggots out there, it's from Stephen Sondheim's *Follies*.

## <u>one more thing</u>

This is me. I will be popping up occasionally, making little comments or illustrating points. I have five pierces in my left ear. I have one pierce in my right nostril. I find this nose pierce particularly helpful in providing an extra breathing hole for cunnilingus.

My hair is short and spiky. This is to throw people off.

"Is that a boy or a girl?"

Every day of my life some person refers to me as a sir. The worst time was in the gynecologist's office.

"We have the results of your Pap smear, sir."

My gyno is one of those really helpful doctors. She tells you everything she's doing when she does it, as if you had no idea. As if you popped up in the stirrups to go for a pony ride.

"Okay," helpful Doc says, "now we're inserting the speculum."

"Thanks, Doc," I think. "I was sure you were going in my who-who with a frozen banana."

"Now we're opening you up and, oh," the gynecologist tour guide confirms, "isn't that a healthy pink cervix! Would you like me to get a mirror so you can see it?"

I reply, "No, thanks. I don't even like to look at my face in a mirror." I would cease visiting this gyno, except for one small detail . . . I *love* her. Her appointments can be very stimulating. She has Parkinson's disease.

I am holding in my hand a Hitachi Magic Wand, the Mercedes-Benz of vibrators. I don't know why. It's not because I'm sexually crazed . . . even though there isn't enough power in my apartment to run my vibrator and I have to run a big orange extension cord out my bedroom window to the generator at the Union Square subway stop. When I jerk off, the number 6 train doesn't run.

## RULE #1

While attending lesbian functions, do not stand up and announce, "I don't know what it is, girls. I just eat and eat and never gain an ounce."

# Ten Commandments for Modern Day

## the [original] ten commandments

1. I am the Lord thy God, thou shalt not have strange gods before me.

2. Thou shalt not take the name of the Lord thy God in vain.

3. Remember the Lord's day and keep it holy.

4. Honor thy father and thy mother.

5. Thou shalt not kill.

6. Thou shalt not commit adultery.

7. Thou shalt not steal.

8. Thou shalt not bear false witness against thy neighbor.

9. Thou shalt not covet thy neighbor's goods.

10. Thou shalt not covet thy neighbor's wife.

The Ten Commandments have been around since, well . . . Moses. This makes the Ten Commandments archaic. As a stand-up comic I find this fact disturbing. If I used material this old I'd be working the Catskills, which would be fine with me if and only if I would have occasion to bump into Jennifer Grey.*

*Jennifer Grey, where are you? What has happened to you? Why oh why are you reduced to working on that trash show? *It's like, you*

Why do Christians believe they can use these archaic rules? Years progress; our criteria for morality should follow suit. I'm certain the Ten Commandments had their place when our mode of dress was slightly above sheepskin loincloths and we were required to procreate through a hole in a sheet. But now we dress in cow skin and procreate in a petri dish.

These thoughts occur to me after having just seen the Virgin Mary's face appear in my morning coffee. I am fairly certain it was the Blessed Mother. But I take my coffee black. It could have been Nipsey Russell.

I, Lea DeLaria, nice Italian Catholic girl, have been chosen to redraft the Ten Commandments to function in our Cyber Fuck world. You can rest assured that the Modern-Day Ten Commandments to follow are clear and concise, and come complete with "Loose Translations." These translations will serve as descriptive explanatory notes, alleviating all confusion as to their meaning.

LOOSE TRANSLATION: You can't fuck them up.

If you do not follow these Modern-Day Ten Commandments, you will burn in hell . . . sorry, the BVM just scolded me. Mary says to do your best. Mary has obviously had some recent experience with a twelve-step program.

### <u>original commandment number one</u>

**I am the Lord thy God, thou shalt not have strange gods before me.**

This commandment is clearly in need of modification. Right-wing Christians have conjured up the oddest gods

---

*know?* If you need the money that badly, I have the perfect job in mind for you. It pays very well and I provide the schoolgirl uniform.

the world has ever known. Pat Robertson's god rained fires on half of Florida because, according to Pat, God was showing dissatisfaction over a single Florida city allowing the unfurling of Gay Pride flags. Pat's god is not only off, Pat's god is suffering from P.M.S.

In the spirit of true Christianity, Original Commandment Number One will be replaced.

### modern-day commandment number one

**Remember, keep thy Lord to thyself!**

In the spirit of Original Commandment Number One, you get to keep right on believing in your Lord or God or higher power or lavender spirit. However, due to the highly manipulated end-product of the Christian right, you are no longer allowed to spew about it on national television or anywhere else where someone who might disagree with you could possibly hear. Including the subway, the mall, any gay-rights anything, the sidewalk, and most especially the corner of Forty-ninth Street and Broadway at 2:00 P.M. on Sunday afternoon, when every queer dancer on Broadway, meaning every dancer on Broadway, is just trying to get over their Saturday night hangover enough to get through the matinee.

I was one such queer passing by this insufferable White Christian Creep screaming scripture as his black . . . well . . . slave (!?!) handed out Creepy Christian Crap. At the high point of Paul chapter one verse eleven the White Christian Creep was overcome by his rapture. He was only able to express himself by screaming, "God. God. God. Oh God. Oh God. Oh my God. God. God." I listened for a bit and remarked, "It's funny, sir, but you sound just like the girl I was banging not five hours ago."

Some of you might have First Amendment concerns over my Modern-Day Commandment Number One. Mary and I would like to respond. Too fucking bad. Call the ACLU. They would be pleased as punch to bring a lawsuit on your behalf. You're going to have a tough time finding a defendant. I'm just the messenger, and the Virgin Mary just disappeared from my cup on her way to who knows where. You might find out by dialing 1–900–ASK–MARY.*

Jesus said in the Sermon on the Mount, "Beware the man who makes a show of his religion. He does it for himself and not for God."

LOOSE TRANSLATION: Don't go on *The 700 Club* and guilt-trip widows into signing over their Social Security checks, which you'll use to hold a prayer meeting in Palm Springs with your big-titted, Jersey-haired secretary/personal assistant.

If you are going to use the Bible then use *all* of it. It is henceforth verboten to quote only the sections of Leviticus that further your pea-brained agenda. Don't tell me not to have a mouth full of woman when you've got a mouth full of pulled pork.

And another thing. You are no longer allowed to mix politics with religion. We've let you go on this for a long time, and they are still fighting in the Middle East.

Jesus had charisma. No one had more charisma than Jesus. If Jesus didn't run for office then neither should Oral Roberts or Jesse Jackson or L. Ron Hubbard, whose Scientology preaches that we humans have not accessed our entire brains. If we had, we would know that each and every one of us carries implanted in our gray matter a particle of an alien race, the thetans. The thetans, L. Ron believed and

*Doesn't 1–900–ASK–MARY sound like an advice column for fags?

taught, colonized Earth but were destroyed by a volcano, which scattered their ashes. Here's the tricky part: The scattered ashes became a part of our planet's mud, the mud from which we evolved.

Mr. Hubbard, exactly how much of your brain did you access to come up with that tax deduction?

### original commandment number two

**Thou shalt not take the name of
the Lord thy God in vain.**

Well, Jesus H. Fucking Christ on a raft giving head to the Pope. I don't know what to say about this one.

It is clear to all who walk the Earth that Original Commandment Number Two has lost its clout. Original Commandment Number Two belongs in a Commandment museum. Who does not say "Goddamnit" when they stub their toe or trip over a kid's toy or miss the coke dealer on rave night? There are more uses for the Lord's name in vain than there are members of the King family.

### modern-day commandment number two

**Thou shalt not take the name of
Susan Sarandon in vain.**

Damn! Does this fine bitch drink the blood of virgins or what? Oh . . . sorry . . . there I go again. Allow me to explain: As the messenger bringing you the Modern-Day Ten Commandments, I, and I alone, may break them every now and then. It was Mary who informed me of this, not two minutes ago. She made a return appearance in the fog of my bathroom mirror . . . or was that Cher? I so often confuse the two.

The rockin' babe that is Susan Sarandon is just like a fine red wine. As she matures, her aroma opens to reveal a spicy flavor with excellent legs. Parker and I give her four stars.

From the first time I saw her in her panties in *The Rocky Horror Picture Show* to the last time I saw her in her panties in my dressing room . . . okay, Mary, that was a lie . . .

If I was married to the most perfect woman in the world and the opportunity arose to "do" Susan Sarandon, an exception would have to be made.

LOOSE TRANSLATION: You are now allowed a list made up of people you have no chance of ever bedding regardless of your fantasies. If by some remote happenstance, like say a roofie falls into their cocktail and some of them ends up on your face, it does not count as an affair. Susan Sarandon is at the top of this list.

You are allowed to comprise your own list, provided you do not break Modern-Day Commandment Number Two. You must start your list with "Susan Sarandon." After that, you're on your own. Still, Mary says, as your messenger I must give you guidance on how to compose your list so you do not get lost along the way. Therefore, here's my list of women it's okay to sleep with and it's not adultery.

## <u>lea's list of women it's okay to<br>sleep with and it's not adultery</u>

### 1. Susan Sarandon

### 2. Sigourney Weaver

### 3. Ingrid Casares
**(Oops, this is supposed to be a list of people you have no chance of getting.)**

### 3. Lauryn Hill

4. Uma Thurman

5. Natalie Portman

6. Sandra Bernhard

7. Isabella Rossellini

8. Cate Blanchett

9. Lara Flynn Boyle

10. Any girl in a kilt studying history

## original commandment number three

**Remember the Lord's day and keep it holy.**

What day would the Lord's day be again? Would it be Sunday? Because I think most people get paid double overtime to work on Sundays. I suppose the bosses must have had a little chat with Satan on this one and figured that twice as much money was what it would take for most people to risk burning in hell. Is anything closed on Sundays anymore? When I was growing up we had these things called "Blue Laws." I never did know why they called them that except the liquor stores were closed on Sundays, which I suppose made everyone blue. Pa. Dum. Pum.

Some religions observe the Sabbath on Saturday. That's convenient, not to mention job-limiting.

"Sorry, sir, I can't work on Saturdays."

"Next."

Okay, so Original Commandment Number Three is as stale as David Brenner's act. There is no day of rest, so get over it. In fact, Original Commandment Number Three is hereby completely replaced and revamped to deal with the modern-day problem of road rage. There is a method to our madness here. By dealing with road rage in Modern-Day Commandment Number Three, we will be helping you with Modern-Day Commandment Number Five, which as you will see is not that much different from Original Commandment Number Five, which has to do with killing-n-stuff. So Mary says to just trust us.

### modern-day commandment number three

**Do not do any of the following annoying driving things:**

## A. Do Not:
## Park Your Speed-Limit-Following Ass in the Fast Lane.

Now, this is a very serious modern-day problem and one of the chief causes of highway homicide. Most especially when you park your speed-limit-following ass in the fast lane and stay there, even though I, who have the horsepower and the *cojones* to go 90 or 100 miles per hour, come up behind you and want to pass. You don't move. I make an attempt to pass you on the right. You start a drag race. I give up and decelerate. You put on your plastic sheriff's badge and decide that no one on the freeway is allowed to go faster than you. What, Mommy took her teat away too soon, so no one arrives at work on time?

## B. Do Not:
## Own a Minivan.

I am aware of minivans being the answer to the question of transporting a team full of soccer kids. However, the minivan clientele who operate these automotive abominations have no clue as to the size of their vehicles. Yes, it drives like a car. Yes, it rides like a car.

No, it is not a car. It is a van. It is a small van. Hence the name "minivan." People who trade in their car for a van seem to have forgotten a basic principle: You must first learn to drive a van. Until you do you are not allowed to own a minivan unless it comes loaded with an option that ejects your obnoxious kids out the rear when you get hit from behind.

## C. Do Not:
## Turn in Front of My Car from a Side Street at the Very Last Minute.

Now, this is the most dangerous subsection of Modern-Day Commandment Number Three to overlook. Literally. You inevitably cause me to slam on my brakes and swerve around your yummy lime-green '87 Hyundai, which, by the way, you were supposed to throw away after three years. To add insult to injury, almost every time this happens I glance in my rearview mirror to see not one vehicle remotely behind me. Hey, Mikey, did you just get your license and you're in a hurry to show the gang at the Dairy Queen? Not an excuse.

## D. Do Not:
## Put a Plastic Mary Statue on Your Dashboard.

This just pisses Mary off. She hasn't seen one that looks like her yet, and she wants to know why it is you people think she only wears that same damn blue dress. She may have been a virgin, but that doesn't mean she didn't like to look nice.

LOOSE TRANSLATION: Mary says if you ever, ever, ever break any part of Modern-Day Commandment Number Three, she will appear in your rearview mirror and cause you to have a traffic accident that will wipe out everyone you've ever loved and a school bus full of "special kids" and everyone will die horrific deaths but you. You will survive to see it all happening at a speed that seems equal to the one you were driving at when you broke Modern-Day Commandment Number Three Subsection A. Mary says she'll make sure you blow an over-the-limit alcohol content, which means you'll go to jail for the rest of your life and end up the bitch wife of a man called Junior.

## original commandment number four

### Honor thy father and thy mother.

Now, there is absolutely nothing wrong with this Commandment. Except that no one pays any attention to it whatsoever. It's as if they take one look at it and say, "Hey, how can I screw my parents over the most? Shoot up a school yard and then kill myself?"

Or how about, "Cut myself off from my mom, live in a hut as a recluse, and send bombs to people I've never met but think might be dangerous to the survival of the world? Oh yeah, and then get caught so my mom has to live through my trial."

Or better yet, "Wear my pants so big that they hang off my ass so low that it looks like I'm perpetually taking a huge dump?"

What's next? Jerry Springer? Well no, Jerry Springer is not next, because of Modern-Day Commandment Number Four.

## modern-day commandment number four

### Honor thy father and thy mother
### while on national TV.

Trust me, your life is uninteresting. You must know that. Isn't that precisely why you agreed to go on a nationally televised talk show and make an ass of yourself and your entire family in the first place? This is unacceptable, unless, of course, you're going to talk about Mary, who has apparently left the building but told me to warn you about the talk show thing before she disappeared from my blue toilet bowl.

So the next time Jerry Springer or Ricki Lake or Sally Jessy shows up at your trailer park and asks, "Who inbreeds here? We need a guest," you must resist. After all, your parents are retired now and will see your toothless face on television when the show airs during the middle of the day.

Frankly, Mary and I don't care what you think until you learn how to floss.

LOOSE TRANSLATION: Learn dental hygiene. Get a great smile. Make your parents proud.

### original commandment number five

**Thou shalt not kill.**

Well, we all know how messed up this Commandment is by the amount of "Christians" who support the death penalty and think it's okay to wage "holy wars." Wrong. There is no subsection to Original Commandment Number Five saying "Thou shalt not kill . . . except in the following circumstance." Of course there is the old "eye for an eye," which predates the Original Ten Commandments by some thousand years. Sorry, Peter Falk. An "eye for an eye" doesn't mean you're really supposed to take an eye for an eye. It is just a figure of speech, a biblical era cliché, like the missionary position.

Having said that, it's clear that certain things have

become more important than life itself, and one of those things seems to be time. People are always complaining how they'd kill for more time in the day or more time with their kids or more time just to "hang out." Therefore, time, having become more important than death, must never be killed. Hence, Original Commandment Number Five is hereby replaced with:

## modern-day commandment number five

**Thou shalt not kill time . . .**

### A. In a Starbucks.

I remember the good old days when I used to read Nietzsche in the library. Now all I see are these affected little fucks who sit in Starbucks giving me attitude, which is exactly what I need from a white person with dreadlocks.

"Hey, you in the tie-dye, here's a quarter, go buy yourself a culture."

And exactly how many Starbucks does it take to satisfy the savory coffee needs of America? Huh? How many fucking Starbucks? My guess is we'll never know, because they're putting another one in down the block kitty-corner to the one they built last month. Heaven forbid you should have to cross the fucking street for a Starbucks. It wouldn't be so offensive if their coffee actually tasted like coffee instead of what comes out the runoff tube from a mortician's table. No matter, though, because by the time they actually serve it to you you're *on* the mortician's table.

LOOSE TRANSLATION: If you actually have enough time to sit in a Starbucks and read Nietzsche, you need to take your overprivileged white ass down to a shelter or someplace like that and help someone less fortunate than

you. Plus, Mary says you shouldn't be reading that motherfucker. He really dissed her relatives.

## B. In an Airplane.

Now, killing time in an airplane can be done in a myriad of
ways, the first of which is by mistaking your Buick for a
carry-on. This, of course, causes you to take the entire time
designated to fly to the destination to attempt to shove
your Buick in the overhead compartment while the rest of
us stand in what appears to be a bread line in Moscow.
Time manslaughter. Not okay.

Another assault on time in an airplane comes when you
set up your office in the emergency exit row. As if your fat,
I've-been-sitting-behind-a-desk-for-the-last-twenty-five-
years butt isn't taking up enough room. No, you have to get
the aisle seat and bring your briefcase, set up your laptop,
your fax machine, your copy machine, and your secretarial
pool, so that I, who's been unfortunate enough to be seated
in the middle seat next to you, have to squeeze into the ash-
tray that has been hermetically sealed to stop people from
smoking. Why am I always stuck next to these gentlemen?
Just once I would like to board a plane to find I'm seated
next to Jodie Foster, who turns to me and says, "Flying
makes me airsick and the only thing that cures it is cunnilingus. Can you help?"

LOOSE TRANSLATION: If the flight is short, board
fast, sit down, and shut up. If the flight is long, board fast,
sit down, take a Xanax, and shut up.

### original commandment number six

**Thou shalt not commit adultery.**

Ha, ha, ha, ha, ha, ha, ha! I'm sorry, I just can't stop laughing. Let me catch my breath.

Original Commandment Number Six has been proven, by our very own President William Jefferson "Jack me off, no don't, okay do, no don't, okay do" Clinton, to be impenetrable. Pun intended. Now, everyone, including God, knows how you can have sex without having sex, and therefore not commit adultery. And that is exactly the problem with Original Commandment Number Six. It is overly broad. It leaves way too much to interpretation. Here is a true story:

## a true story

I once knew a man who felt he wasn't committing adultery if he didn't sleep over after boinking his mistress. He believed this with all of his little heart and soul. He thought he had found the adultery loophole amongst the other holes. Pa. Dum. Pum. Ching.

Another person I knew, a woman who was married to a man and gleefully carrying on with a woman, told me that it says in the Talmud that a woman who is married to a man and having an affair with an unmarried woman is not committing adultery.

So what is adultery? If you are unmarried can you commit adultery? Does adultery then not apply to us queer types? Are gays and lesbians adultery-proof people? Mary does not think so.

## modern-day commandment number six

**Thou shalt not commit adult-ery.**

I think what you are thinking is, "That's the same as Original Commandment Number Six."

No. By adding the very clever hyphen, I morph the sexual connotation of adultery into a whole new meaning. The definition of adult-ery is "behaving like an adult."

"Lea, you're thirty-two now.* Isn't it time you grew up and started acting like an adult?"

The only sentence worse than the adult-ery sentence is this: "Lea, it's Strom Thurmond. I'm naked and ready for you in the bedroom."

This adult-ery nonsense is surely thinly veiled snobbery directed at my penchant for dating girls half my age.** I know some individuals believe I should leave off partying with people ten years younger than my thirty-five-year-old self.*** Perhaps these same individuals find it unseemly that anyone my age goes out dancing all night, ingesting Ecstasy, and drinking myself into a blackout, only to come to at five o'clock in the morning at a McDonald's and discover I'm employed there.

Shouldn't life be exciting? Sometime ago I was flirting with a gaggle of cute girls. I call them "girls," as they had not been on this planet as long as my thirty-three years.**** I was busy being charming, trying to decide which one I'd like to slip inside, when the original hottie, meaning the one who pulled me over to the gaggle, began to regale us with a tale:

## a hottie tale

It seems our hero hottie had been out dancing the previous night. She was sweaty on the floor enjoying her gyrations when she noticed she was being cruised.

* My age according to *The New York Times*.
** Forty, according to *People* magazine.
*** My age according to *Elle* magazine.
**** My age according to *Rolling Stone* magazine.

"Who wouldn't cruise you?" I think. "Ray Charles?"

The extremely hot hottie continues making it clear that it wasn't being cruised that surprised her, it was the cruiser. The cruiser was a dark mysterious woman wearing a hooded purple cape. The gaggle of hotties giggled. Gaggle? What is a better word for a group of young beautiful lesbians? Perhaps . . . a lick? So to make a long story endless, the lick of hotties began to giggle, the purple cape being the amusing part. Then the original hottie, the tongue of the lick, told us the mysterious woman in the hooded purple cape asked her to dance. She declined. The lick clucked and approved of her decision. I did not.

"Life," I said, "presents us with a myriad of strange and exciting possibilities."

The lick looked somewhat confused. I pushed on.

"Life presents these possibilities exactly once." The lick continued to look collectively unsure of my point, proving to be cute but not astute. I clarified.

"If I have a motto in life it is this: Always dance with the lady in the purple cape."

All right, then. Everyone who believes dating out of your generation is:

a. A control thing

b. A midlife crisis

c. Insecurity with oneself

d. Escaping death

e. Just about the tits and ass

please form a military-straight line, bend over, pucker up, and kiss my hairy dyke ass.

## kissing my hairy dyke ass

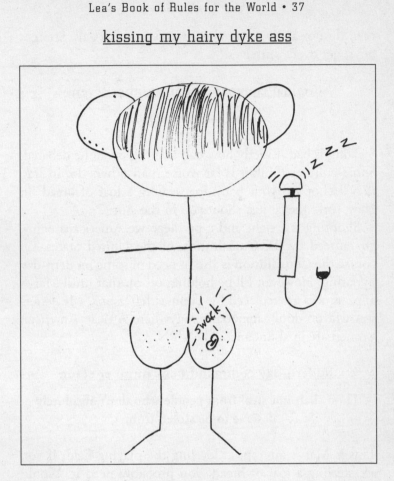

Okay . . . some of it is about the tits and ass. That doesn't change the fact that you are jealous. You know it. I know it. Straight boys can't handle it when a woman gets more pussy than they do . . . and I'm the one who's supposed to grow up. Nope. Forget it. Not going to happen. Move along. Nothing to see here. You don't have to go home. You just have to go.

LOOSE TRANSLATION: All the rules that apply to

men do not apply to butches. That's it. That's all. Straight boys, get over yourselves.*

### original commandment number seven

**Thou shalt not steal.**

Stealing is bad. Exactly how bad stealing is can be debated. Some cultures think it is far worse than others do. In Iraq they'll chop off your hand for stealing a loaf of bread. In New York, they'll just shoot you in the store.

Shooting is a right and a privilege we Americans enjoy, guaranteed by the Constitution of the United States. Of course the Constitution is also in need of some modern-day updating. However, I'll be holding off on that until Mary's appearances are replaced by Thomas Jefferson's. Mr. Jefferson will no doubt materialize anywhere African-American women are in abundance, like UPN. . . .

### modern-day commandment number seven

**Thou shalt not steal from people who don't absolutely deserve to be stolen from.**

This is Mary's attempt at leveling the playing field. If you are stealing a loaf of bread, you probably need it. Would God be mad at you for this? Modern-Day Commandment Number Seven now allows those in dire need to steal, and those not in dire need to steal from those who have way, way, way too much. Provided, of course, you give most of that away to people who need it more than you do. You are

---

* How old am I? I recently had a birthday. I turned actor thirty.

allowed to keep a percentage, because fair is fair and everyone should be paid for their work. We are not Communist.

LOOSE TRANSLATION: It's grammar-school-simple, really. Robin Hood for the modern day. Steal from Bill Gates and give to, well, anyone, because everyone has less money than Bill Gates.

## original commandment number eight

**Thou shalt not bear false witness
against thy neighbor.**

This commandment is simply incomprehensible. What does "false witness against one's neighbor" mean? The nuns inform us it means we should not lie. How are we to know that? When I read Original Commandment Number Eight, I think it is okay to lie as long as you don't about your neighbor. This is virtually impossible for me. I live in New York.

It is clear there was never a "Thou shalt not lie" commandment. All you lawyers can start lamenting your waste of time nit-picking over exactly what word means what so you can answer a question untruthfully without actually lying under oath.

## modern-day commandment number eight

**Thou shalt not bear false breast.**

I understand that this male-oriented society has an ultimate standard of beauty based on large breast.

I myself love large breast. They are soft and sensual and

usually very responsive to touch, tongue, and teeth. I love large breast especially when they are actual human tissue.

Fake breast tend to be rock hard. You can actually bounce a quarter off of a fake boob and poke out somebody's eye. Silicone implants ride high on a woman's body.

"What's that on your forehead? It looks like . . . nipples?"

These implants are also very sturdy, almost stoic. The things don't move. This may seem old-fashioned, but when I suck a tit, I don't want it to suck back. Even Pamela Anderson Lee saw this one coming. Repent, resist, remove those plastic anchors . . . and, ladies, please call me as soon as you do.

LOOSE TRANSLATION: To repent successfully under Modern-Day Commandment Number Eight, Mary insists you remove all fake tissue and pass inspection. Think of it as one of those state car inspection places. You may hate to go, but you have to. Especially if you ever want to get that sticker on your windshield that, besides saying you're a good car doobee, keeps asshole cops from pulling you over for no other reason than, well, you look like me, or yeah, you have a little more melanin in your complexion.

Anyway, the only difference between the car inspection place and the boob inspection place is that the uppity state bureaucrat with attitude as big as her hair is replaced by an official boob inspector, and the only official boob inspector is . . . you guessed it.

## official authorized boob inspection booth

## original commandments numbers nine and ten

**Thou shalt not covet thy neighbor's goods.**

**Thou shalt not covet thy neighbor's wife.**

Mary and I have combined Original Commandments Numbers Nine and Ten, for obvious reasons. They both deal with "coveting." Actually they both deal with coveting things that "belong" to your neighbor. So the wife *belongs* to the neighbor. Isn't this where Lily Tomlin gets pissed and walks off the set?

It's obvious to me that coveting your neighbors' stuff has not only become rampant, it's an American tradition. We've been keeping up with the Joneses so long that we've passed them and moved on to just Jonesing the Joneses.

And as for your neighbor's wife: You left her home alone during the day. Is it my fault she needed help with some heavy lifting around the house?

## modern-day commandment number nine

### Thou shalt not fuck too much with thy neighbor's:

### A. Phone Machine.

Which means, asshole, you don't call someone's house and repeat over and over, "I know you're there. Pick up, pick up, pick up, pick up," like a parrot on crystal meth. There is only one exception to this rule, and that is if you are calling your girlfriend of thirteen years who has just dumped you for a twenty-two-year-old. Then the behavior is a prerequisite.

As to outgoing messages, you are no longer to say, "Wait for the beep." Most of us have been dealing with phone machines our entire adult lives. Why not just remind us to blink.

## a stupid caller's brush with technology

Ring. Ring. Ring.

**PHONE MACHINE**
You've reached 979 . . .

**STUPID CALLER**
Hey! It's me! Are you home? I know you're there!
Pick up. Pick up. Pick up. Pick up. Pick up. Okay. I
guess I missed you.

Click.

**PHONE MACHINE**
. . . wait for the beep.

Beep.

### B. E-Mail.

I get tons of e-mail I don't want, from people I don't know. "How to get rich," "How to get thin," "Welcome to the

Dungeon of Tit Clamps." What is the "Dungeon of Tit Clamps"? A place that only sells tit clamps. Do not ask me how I got this information.

The only thing worse than unwanted e-crap is chain e-mail from someone who claims to be your friend. This quickly removes you from the Buddy List.

On the bad computer etiquette front, blindly forwarded mail is bad. It is not our friend. Nobody believes the story about the guy from Salt Lake City who got his nose broken after he lit a match so the hamster caught up his boyfriend's ass could find its way out thus igniting gases in boy-toy's colon causing the rodent to be shot like a cannon into his face. Yes, it is funny. Yes, it is completely unbelievable.

If you're going to forward something to me, please make it something factual I can use:

### list of factual things i can use

1. Natalie Portman's telephone number

2. Any dirt on John Travolta's "marriage"

3. Keanu Reeves's filming schedule and instructions on how to build a bomb.*

4. Chelsea Clinton's class schedule

5. Where I left the car keys

When sending factual things I can use, please attach a personal note. I see no reason why it should be so difficult to attach a personal note. I get personal notes from the Dungeon of Tit Clamps: "Lea, don't miss these, they really hurt!" These people are not my friends. All right, most of them aren't.

---

* Look, I'm not a stickler for method acting. I don't think you have to see the trees or the stars, but for God's sake, Keanu, see something!

LOOSE TRANSLATION: Modern-day technology requires modern-day common sense. Use it or your techno-toys will melt in your hands and turn into things that resemble, who else, the Virgin Mary.

### original commandment number ten

**Thou shalt not covet thy neighbor's wife.**

Mary and I aren't stupid. We weren't born yesterday. Actually, Mary, when were you born? No one ever tells that story. How old are you? Mary? Mary? Oh, that Mary, she's disappeared again. She always takes off when I start asking about her age. You know, I don't think Mary wants anyone to know how old she really is because if we start counting backward we could find her a bit too young to . . . well . . . we could certainly blow the roof off this miraculously intact hymen business.

### modern-day commandment number ten

**Thou shalt not covet thy neighbor's wife, unless:**

1. She's really, really cute.

2. She's got big hooters.

3. Your neighbor is your ex.

4. She needs help lifting something heavy around the house.

5. Your neighbor's wife is your ex.

6. She's Susan Sarandon.

There, now you have The Modern-Day Ten Commandments from the only real authorities on modern-day living and Christianity. Mary, the Virgin Mother, and Lea DeLaria, the Mother of Virgins.

Good luck with them, and God bless.

## RULE #2

Never laugh at another
person's dream . . . unless,
of course, the dream is
really fucking retarded.

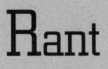

Rant

The year is 1997. The season is summer. The place is the city. *The* City. New York City. I am ensconced in the city, participating in New Yorkers' favorite pastime . . . bitching about tourists. *They're back.* We had enjoyed a short respite from those bridge-and-tunnel cretins. Now they flock to us again, courtesy of our fearless leader Rudolph Giuliani.

Rudy is a Republican. Rudy is a middle-class Republican. Rudy is a middle-class white Republican. Rudy is an antigay, antiporn, antiFUN, middle-class white Republican. Shall we rechristen him Benito Giuliani?

Hizzoner is planning a run for the Senate. His opposing candidate will be none other than First Lady Hillary Clinton. I love Hillary. I find her savvy, charming, expressive, and good for the country. My only hope is that she will use the Senate as a springboard for the Presidency. It would be nice to have a President Clinton who knows how to keep a dick in its place.

However, heaven forbid, if anything should happen and our Hillary decides not to run, leaving the state Democrats without a candidate . . . well, I volunteer. I would be happy to run against Benito. I already have my campaign slogan.

If I had the honor of running the greatest city in the world I assure you I would not revitalize it by systematically removing all of its charm.

What is New York City without a wild cab ride? No more. Now it's Cindy Adams, Paul Sorvino, or Sally: "Hi, New York. It's Sally Jessy Raphael. Buckle up, you're riding through the greatest city on Earth . . . and if you find a pair of red glasses back there, they're mine."

If you find those red glasses do give them back, because poor Sally now must wear her green ones and no one can recognize her. While I'm on the topic . . . Sally, why did you leave your glasses in the backseat? What possible circumstance could cause you to do such a thing? Did you not have the fare for the nice taxi man? Did you offer instead to give him a blow job? Did you therefore remove your glasses to comply? Sally, is it you stuck between the seats blowing that nasty air through that little vent or am I smelling what Mohammed is eating while he drives?

If I were mayor, Times Square would be Times Square, instead of an ad for Disney World. Remember the guy who used to stand on the northeast corner of Forty-second and Eighth muttering, "Live sex, live sex, live sex"? Was he looking for live sex or offering live sex? I asked him once. "What about live sex?" said I, "because I'm all for it."

If you remember him, you know he was attractive in that *Midnight Express* meets *Midnight Cowboy* sort of way. He finished his cigarette and continued his muttering. It took a moment before I realized he was answering my question.

"You give me twenty bucks. I get three other people to give me twenty bucks. Then I take the four of you into a room at the Carter Hotel and you watch two people fuck. No touching."

Excuse me? All right, I admit I enjoy milling about Times Square, which is possibly the sleaziest square in our round world, and yes, once I did finger a girl in a doorjamb around the corner. However, I draw the line when it comes to actually entering a room in the Carter Hotel. The Carter Hotel is almost as bad as the Milford Plaza . . . and in the center of it all is the Milford Plaza . . .

That horrid commercial spins incessantly in your brain as soon as you hear the words "Milford Plaza" . . . *and in the center of it all is the Milford Plaza* . . .

I was once asked to spend the night in the Milford Plaza . . . *and in the center of it*—SHUT UP SHUTUPSHUTUP SHUTUPSHUTUP . . . thank you.

I proceeded to my room. *Squish, squish, squish.* There is

a particular face one makes at a Cambodian restaurant when offered the specialty of the house, Bar-b-qued Pidgeon Head. I was making that particular face as I listened to the *squish squish squish* of my Doc Martens boots on what I hope is *not* semen-soaked seventies carpet.

I arrived at my room to discover missing bedclothes. No pillowcases. No top sheet. No bottom sheet. There was a mattress. There is only one way to describe this mattress. Have you seen the movie *Carrie*?

After I checked out I spent the next several hours in Grand Central Station waiting for the first metro train to New Haven. Better the possibility of forced fellatio on an unwashed indigent than the actuality of spending the night at the Milford Plaza . . . *and in the center* . . .

## milford plaza overload

* * *

The live sex guy is gone now, along with the pimps and whores, junkies and drug dealers. There are no more gay movie houses to catch cinematic treasures like *Box Lunch* or *Schindler's Fist.*

Now every bridge-and-tunnel cretin who owns a car drives around and around the Broadway neighborhood. They just go in circles, as it is against the law in their state, the nuclear waste state, to take a left turn, ergo they are incapable of making one. So if you are strolling through Giuliani's Pride and you observe a Jersey plate using its left signal, do yourself a favor and run like hell. The bastard's coming on the sidewalk.

I've just narrowly avoided a sporty Yugo by leaping up on an expired parking meter, when my good friend Greg Butler walks by. Greg is a six feet four, bald, muscular African American with a six-pack on his stomach you could break bricks on. He really works that Mandingo thing. Walking into a bar with Greg is like walking into heaven with God.

I remove myself from the pole, which is thankfully not inserted anywhere embarrassing, and greet my friend.

"Mother Teresa just died," says Greg, visibly upset.

"What!" I exclaim. "How can that be? Mother Teresa, snatched from us in the prime of her life." Let's face it, by the time the good mother finally passed, it seemed like the good sisters pushing her chair were wheeling around a piece of beef jerky.

My friend, undaunted by my sarcasm, which is why he is my friend, continues his personal death knell. "Everything happens in threes: Princess Di, Mother Teresa, Versace."

Versace? What is that *Sesame Street* song? Oh yes, "One of These Things Is Not Like the Other."

Why would any self-respecting fag mourn the death of Mother Teresa? Certainly she fed the hungry masses and probably saved many lives, but what did the human Raisinet ever do for me and mine except spout the fallacy that according to Jesus, homosexuality is against the family? Has anyone ever examined Jesus' family? The guy hung out with twelve men, a known prostitute, and a donkey. Furthermore, I am quite certain all four gospels quote him as saying to those twelve men, "This is my body. Eat me."

How can anyone look at Mother Teresa and not see the whole of her work? Suppose I say to you, "The Shah of Iran was one of the world's biggest fascists. He orchestrated the deaths of over eight million people, but you should have seen him play basketball when he went for a three pointer. Nothin' but net." Would you accept that? Of course you would, because humans have the infuriating ability to swallow the largest piles of crap simply to avoid being impolite. This phenomenon is directly related to white society's incredibly WASPy attitude toward rage: "You're having a feeling. Go to your room."

Once upon a time, in a very radical West Coast town, I found myself spewing my venom in my own unique way. "Aren't you glad the man who said catsup is a vegetable is now a vegetable himself?" said I. Imagine my surprise to find myself standing in front of what I thought to be like-minded people, listening to them boo. Was I being mean? I think not. I have no trouble hating the man who is single-handedly responsible for the deaths of eighty-seven of my friends over a fourteen-year period. You do the math. ASSHOLES GET ALZHEIMER'S TOO should be the bumper sticker.

I don't sound like a post-Ellen homogenized lesbian. The reason for that is simple. I was a lesbian long before Ellen, and like Ellen, I can't stand referring to myself as a "lesbian." We have both expressed distaste toward that word. Ellen hates "lesbian" because she thinks "it sounds like a disease." Okay, boys and girls, can you say "internalized homophobia"? I knew you could. I won't call myself a lesbian, because it sounds like someone you call to repair things in your home. "Honey, the air conditioner is on the blink. Better call the lesbian."

I prefer "dyke," even if by doing so I inadvertently ally myself with healingsistermountainwomanrain feminists. I mean the ones who paint themselves lavender, dance naked around tiered fires, and have beards.* I want to secretly follow behind them like a stealth bomber and whisper things like "Tweezers."

I want to say something to these girls, and don't you just know I love referring to these babes as "girls" . . . and "babes," for that matter. Girls, it is the year 2000, there's a hole in the ozone, war ravages our planet, and the Congress of the United States spent forty million dollars of our tax money to determine whether or not the President got a blow job when we could have bought him four blow jobs for two hundred bucks. At least then we'd know he had one. Actually, why didn't we know it already? He is the President of the United States; of course he gets blow jobs. It is part of the presidential job description:

### presidential job description

**Most powerful man in the world. Comes with unlimited blow jobs.**

---

* Has anyone else noticed that the ones with the beards are usually fire-eaters. Can't they find a less hazardous pastime, like transporting nitro?

Accept it. All presidents get blow jobs. George Bush got blow jobs. Okay. That's a picture I want out of my head immediately.

Simply put, the world is falling apart. So if you think worshipping some fat-assed goddess is going to help, you go right ahead. I don't have the time. I already know how to spell "woman" and unfortunately sometimes it is spelled i-d-i-o-t. If you wish to wear some huge gaudy natural crystal on your heart chakra like some kind of voodoo rite that keeps you in tune with the energy of the universe . . . have at it. Just don't expect the same from me, because, honey, I think it's a rock. By the way, if that rock's transmission of the karmic energy of the universe is supposed to make your life better, then why do you live in a van?

I have my own version of karma: DeLaria Karma, or De-Lariarma, which is similar to yours, except instead of natural crystals I use an Uzi.

DeLariarma works with the use of a powerful mantra: "You hate me so I hate you. You hate me so I hate you."

DeLariarma creates a hyperawareness of one's total surroundings, making everything go up your butt, no lube.

### examples of things that go up my butt, no lube

1. Why is there Prozac for dogs? How can you have the ability to lick yourself and still be depressed?

2. While in court fighting a ticket she received for single driving in the carpool lane, a woman recently informed the judge that her fine should be canceled

because she was pregnant at the time. Does this mean that I can drive in the carpool lane if I'm possessed by Satan?

3. What exactly is *minor* feminine itching? Is that when you don't want to rip it off and throw it across the street?

4. "*My-T-Fine*" dog food and "*K*razy Glue." And we wonder why Johnny can't spell.

5. The NRA. I was once in favor of strict gun control, but now I believe we should wait until Charlton Heston has a fatal accident with his own handgun. *Then* we ban them.*

6. Department of Defense. Apparently there was hubbub at the Pentagon over some zealous soldier writing "thoughtless graffiti" on bombs being dropped on Kosovo. Which one do you think is more rude? Graffiti? Or a two-thousand-pound laser-guided bomb in the middle of your Ramadan dinner party?

7. Sequels. Rod Steiger wants to do a sequel to *The Wizard of Oz*. As a gay person, I must protest anyone tampering with *The Wizard of Oz*. These sorts of projects are doomed from the beginning. Remember the sequel to *Gone With the Wind*? Neither do I.

8. Jewel.

---

* Mr. Heston was recently quoted, "Somewhere in the busy pipeline of public funding is sure to be a demand from a disabled lesbian on welfare that the Metropolitan Opera stage her version of *Carmen*, translated into Ebonics." On second thought, give *me* the gun. I'll shoot him myself.

DeLariarma also works as a character builder. Here's a pertinent example. In number three, why did I, of all people, refer to my vagina as "it"? Am I a self-loathing Christian Barbie doll with the bigger-the-do-the-closer-to-God hair? You know, "ladies say 'down there' "?

Gash, slit, box, the wound that will not heal, my vag, my stuff, my shit, my Sharona, poontang, poonanny, popo, pudendum, couche, cooter, kitty, kitten, beaver, little Lea, gold mine, highway to heaven, pooch, pouch, finger-lickin' good, shnowzer, schnooter, little girl, cookie, le mineau, bucacia, bang box, rug, carpet, stinkhole, jenny, cherry, cherry pie, pie, twat, no-no, front bottom, chicken, peach, juicy fruit, forbidden fruit, leaky wound, bearded clam, bunny, fish, taco, fur burger, who-who, hairpie and when I go down on a woman, I like to call it "looking into the face of God."

Notice. I left out the two big biggies. DeLariarma gives you a flair for the dramatic.

### the two biggies

1. Pussy

2. Cunt

These words will stop conversation even in a hip urban nightclub, the patrons with horrified expressions peering over their latest pink fad drink.

I love these words! I find them incredibly expressive, especially when used in certain contexts, like "My mother's a cunt."*

* I wish to interject here in order to explain the use of the sentence "My mother's a cunt." This sentence is used as a means of humorous illustration. I must state for the record that my mother is most definitely not a cunt. She is more of a pill.

Is "pussy" dirtier than "cunt" or is cunt worse than pussy? Pussy or cunt? Cunt or pussy? Pussy. Pussy. Pussy. Pussy. Cunt. Cunt. Cunt. Cunt. If you are reading this and not practicing DeLariarma you probably think it's too much. I protest. They are normal words. If there is a difference between the two, I expect it is a matter of degrees. You want to fuck a cunt, but you'd like to get to know a pussy.

"You hate me so I hate you. You hate me so I hate you." DeLariarma gives you vocal integrity, i.e., the ability to speak what you believe, no matter who is listening. In April 1993 in Washington, D.C., there was a huge party under the guise of a protest against discrimination continuously perpetuated upon gays and lesbians.

Having made a big splash as the first openly gay comic to appear on television, I became the natural choice to host the shindig.

It was quite a rave. Everyone was there, except Madonna. Where was she? I mean without fags, Madonna would probably be an incredibly bitter waitress in a SoHo brasserie. "No, we don't have Thousand Island, however I can give you a thousand dollops of Roquefort."

Rock stars, TV personalities, and sports figures were all present to espouse their political philosophy, so I felt it was my duty to espouse mine.

"I truly like the Clinton administration," I opined. "Finally we have a first lady you could fuck."

Apparently people believe this is not the sort of statement one should make on the White House steps. These good and decent individuals are forgetting a basic rule.

Allow me to illustrate:

Feminists were particularly enraged. It seems I objectified the First Lady. Apparently my lesbianism does not automatically disqualify me from being a sexist. Phew! Was I glad to hear that, after all these years. Wouldn't it be a drag to discover I've been wasting my time with my *Penthouse* collection, not to mention my copies of *Sorority Sister's Snatch*?

Now, here's the point. DeLariarma, when devoutly practiced, will allow you to grow with your environment.

FACT: It has been several years since the "Hillary" incident.

FACT: I have never forgotten it. Mostly because everyone constantly reminds me, but also because I have grown older and wiser. I realize it is indeed improper for me to sexualize the First Lady, when who I truly want is her daughter.

"You hate me so I hate you. You hate me so I hate you. You hate me so I hate you. You hate me so I hate you." Could I be experiencing a midlife crisis? I've always been attracted to the strong, smart type; Hillary, Sigourney, Cher. Now the Spice Girls seem too . . . well, old. Natalie Portman, Christina Ricci, Drew Barrymore, Liv Tyler; now, that's what I call girl power, like a box of Dunkin' Donuts munchkins. You just want to pop 'em in your mouth, one at a time.

Oh, there goes Lea again. Shooting off her mouth, or in this case, pen. Saying anything to get a rise out of folks, especially folks who think lesbian sexuality should be seen and not heard. In an interview with some gay newspaper, let's call it *Lezzie Rag*, this question was put forth; "What is your guilty pleasure?" I told the truth. Remember? DeLariarma. "Oh, man! I might as well say it: Catholic schoolgirls, about fourteen years old. It's not like I'm a founding member of the North American Woman-Girl Love Association or anything, but I love to look at Catholic schoolgirls in their uniforms."

For the next several months, letters poured into the *Lezzie Rag*, all of them having the same theme: Lea DeLaria is a pedophile.

"You hate me so I hate you. You hate me so I hate you. You hate me so I hate you. You hate me so I hate you."

I'm only going to explain this once. If you are a certain age and you touch in a sexual manner a fourteen-year-old Catholic schoolgirl in uniform, you are a "pedophile." If you are of a certain age and you are sexually attracted to fourteen-year-old Catholic schoolgirls in uniform, you are "alive." Enough said.

## RULE #3

Always refrain from
inserting a finger into
an uncertain hole.

# Xenia and Urbana Go Earthing

"Watch out!" Urbana screams. "You almost hit that asteroid."

Xenia skillfully swerves right, then banks left, continuing on her course.

"Honey, if you insist on screaming every time a bit of space shit comes near us, I'll spin us right back to Venus and we can forget the whole thing."

"Well, I wouldn't be so jumpy if you'd keep your fat eye on the road instead of grooming your tentacles in the backward-viewing device."

"Enough, that's Mir up ahead; we're almost there," Xenia says as she engages the cloaking device.

"God, that thing looks like a piece of crap. How do those Russians keep it up there?"

"Well, it says in this Earth glossy, they keep borrowing from the Canadians."

Xenia expertly glides past Mir and docks their ship into Earth's orbit. She unstraps herself, grabs Urbana by her heads, and proceeds to the communication center. Once there she dials Venus.

After a moment, a sexy voice emanates through the speakers. "Perpie, Terpie, and Zyge, how may I direct your call?"

Urbana puts on her most professional-sounding voice. "May I speak to Terpie, please?"

A voice comes over the speaker. "Terptitudekjdfoingp-sjdijssoigposidjfosjglits speaking."

Urbana excitedly whispers to Xenia, "She must really like us, she's using her nickname."

Xenia ignores Urbana's outburst and speaks directly to Terpie. "Terpie, it's us. Do you have us yet?"

Terpie's holographic image appears in front of Xenia and Urbana. "Ah, there you are, my darlings. You girls are louvernuhts, it makes me wonder if I bought into this travel-packages-to-Earth venture because I thought it was a good idea, or because I was thinking that you two were my choice for werbway of the yor."

Urbana and Xenia have heard this before and laugh extra hard. Terpie annoys them, but they need her Querntinerez.

As always, Xenia starts. "Well, we're here. Do you have any ideas on where we should go?"

Terpie chortles and takes a sip of gloob. "This is your idea, I thought the girls would be into Alpha Centauri this year. Just make my Querns multiply. Triquernillion or more by 3084—that's my motto."

"Remember." She smiles. "The girls on Venus want to get laid, and I mean laid good." Terpie raises an eyebrinkle for effect. "I'm certain you two are experts on this topic. So set it up—although why anyone would want to slerb with Earth lesbians is beyond me. Two eyes? Ewwwwww." Terpie's image begins to fade. "Just make it work, my lovelies . . . or else." On that ominous note, she disappears.

Xenia speaks. "Puleeeeease, she's such a porg. I've never actually seen a man, but I have a feeling Terpie could pass for one on Earth. C'mon, it's time to morph."

Xenia and Urbana set the dial on their Morph-a-matic 3000 to "Earth-Lezzies," and step in. They walk out three seconds later, having achieved their ideal. Xenia and Urbana now appear to be Earth women. Very specific Earth women. They resemble strippers from an upscale girlie joint.

"Urbana, are you sure that *Playboy* magazine is representative of the average Earth-Lezzie?"

"Well, every Earth-Lezzie has one," Urbana replies, checking her data. "Except for the one called 'Chastity Bono.' "

"Okay. Where shall we jump in, then?"

Urbana studies her data.

"Why don't we take in a show?"

Xenia and Urbana clasp hands and dematerialize, instantly reappearing in the back of a Unitarian church hall. They hear laughter and notice a figure on the altar/stage.

"She seems very upset. Why is everyone laughing, Xenia?"

"I don't know, but I wish she'd stand still. Her constant motion is giving me nutroslavalitis."

Xenia, testing her new eyes, rolls them as she speaks. "Puleease, didn't you take your antiorbitron tablets?"

Urbana answers by shaking her human digit for the first time. "There wasn't time. We had to jump in. . . . These . . . fingers? . . . are most expressive."

Xenia, continuing her new facial features test, raises a brow. "That one is going to be the most *missing* if you don't get it out of my nose."

Before the Venusians can square off to test the Earth concept "bitch slap," they are interrupted by the figure on the stage, screaming while downing a shot of vodka.

"Fuck you, Northampton. I'm Lea DeLaria. Good night!"

Xenia and Urbana observe the audience exiting the hall and listen intently to their conversations. Xenia takes notes.

One woman is commenting as she adjusts the strap on

her Birkenstock sandal. "Lea is so vulgar, I don't know why anyone likes her. And the way she drinks onstage . . . I swear I thought I saw her in a meeting once."

Her friend replies, "You're such a prude. I think she's refreshing. Ow, ow, ow, ow, ow, ow. My scarf just got caught in my eyebrow pierce."

Ms. Birkenstock smirks.

"See, the goddess got you."

Xenia and Urbana tilt their heads in a perfect imitation of the RCA dog. "Goddess?" they repeat in unison, and Xenia scribbles in her pad.

Another lesbian passes, buttoning her L.L.Bean coat. "I still think that comment about Hillary Clinton was over the line. And the way she drinks onstage . . . I swear I thought I saw her in a meeting once. . . ."

Xenia and Urbana make a snap decision that this Lea DeLaria woman will make the perfect earthling tour guide. They join hands and transport themselves into Lea's utility closet/dressing room. Lea is bending over doing a line while simultaneously smoking a joint.

Lea can't believe her good fortune. Two such scantily clad ultra-babes appearing in her dressing room out of thin air.

"What the fuck? Please tell me you're not girlfriends, or if you are, please tell me you came to discipline me for swearing in church."

Xenia begins to explain. "Actually, no, Lea. You don't mind if we call you Lea, do you?"

Lea wipes her nose and ogles the aliens' tits.

"Well, I'd prefer you call me Daddy, but Lea's okay." She downs another shot.

Xenia continues, "You see, Urbana and I *are* girlfriends, on a business venture. We come from the planet Venus to set up a tour package so the Venusian woman can come to the planet Earth, mingle with Earth lesbians, and get laid."

The space entrepreneurs finish their frank explanation. Lea hitches the pants of her suit in an all too familiar boy/girl gesture. She lights another joint and takes a big drag.

"Let me get this straight," she says, swallowing a handful of pills with a vodka chaser. "You two are telling me that you are some kind of 'aliens.' " Lea makes the universal sign for quotation marks around the word "alien." "Even though you look like you just stepped off Hugh Hefner's face, you are actually from another planet." She takes another hit from the joint, offering it to the Venusians, who cough and decline. "Another planet, filled with women who look like you and want to come to Earth to fuck dykes."

Xenia and Urbana nod their heads in unison, testing the gesticulation.

"Sounds like Fire Island, only the girls are cute," Lea says, then does a bump of K. "Let's go."

Xenia and Urbana grab Lea's hand and they all dematerialize.

"Where are we?" Lea asks.

Urbana, being the less snobby of the two, replies, "You are in a space-time continuum, which allows us to jump to Earth points via metaphysical planes using the simultaneous universe theorem."

Lea nods. "Cool. I just thought my K kicked in. Then again, it could have been the E."

They reappear at the center of the Michigan Womyn's Music Festival.

"Michigan? You Venus bitches suck. You said I was going to get laid."

Xenia and Urbana look perplexed. Urbana begins to spout datum.

"But according to my information, large clergs of lesbians assemble here annually."

"Yeah, well, you left one thing out of your equation."

"What's that?" Urbana asks.

"I wouldn't fuck any of these babes with someone else's dick. They stink. They've been hanging out in the middle of the fucking woods. Plus, they're complete idiots . . . they're trying to save the whales from a state that only borders on a fucking lake."

Lea notices Ani DiFranco onstage.

"I hate this fucking whiny soprano in A-flat acoustic guitar shit."

Lea shouts toward the stage, "Hey, you, pretentious fuck. Why should I listen to a twentysomething-year-old straight girl tell me what lesbians should do and what lesbians shouldn't do, when you don't even know how to spell 'Annie'! I am so sick of twenty-year-old angst. What do you have to be angst-ridden about? Talk to me when your ass starts to hit you at the back of your knees and you can use your tits to practice hacky sack!"

The crowd interrupts a mantra chant-around and turns on Lea.

"That big dyke's insulting Ani. Let's kill her!"

As the crowd of tree-root-smoking, Isis-loving, wimminloving women advance perilously close to the time-space continuum trio, Lea, who was picking mushrooms during her diatribe, grabs Xenia's and Urbana's hands.

"Get us the fuck out of here before they make us do spin art with our menstrual blood."

As they morph, one lonely cry is heard above the din.

"You called her Annie, and I'm sure it's pronounced Ahh-knee."

"Look," Lea fumes, as they enter a different metaphysical plane, "Urbain, is it?"

Urbana answers, overenunciating for Lea's benefit, "UR BA NA."

"Whatever." Lea begins to pace. "I'm the tour guide and that data you have is about as helpful as Nancy Reagan at a Crisco party. This time we go where I say." Lea starts rooting through her pants pocket in search of something. "Set your TV dial or ray gun or whatever the fuck it is for Thursday night after midnight. We're going to the city, THE CITY, NEW YORK, not Plutoville. The club is Life. The rave is Life's a Bitch. You gotta be like a fuckin' dwarf not to get laid there . . . don't tell Linda Hunt."

As the three begin to jump in, Lea shouts, "Fuck, I dropped all the mushrooms!"

The two space pimps and the one Earth dog land at the height of the party. They glance about, taking in the Sodom and Gomorrah atmosphere. Two go-go dancers simulate cunnilingus as many bored, trendy, urban-type dykes look on. The lights flash and whirl. People scream and gyrate on the dance floor. Straight girls who need to be hip because they have no life or ideas or even fun of their own mingle and kiss each other while horny fraternity boys look on. Everyone is high. Everyone is bi.

"Oh my God!" Urbana cries. "Those women are wearing the same outfits as we are!"

Lea's amused. "Only the drag queens, honey."

Undaunted, Urbana continues.

"But my factoids show—"

"Pu-leeeeease, Urbana, it's clear your factoids don't show crapatoolis. . . ."

As Xenia is speaking, a straight man wearing an Armani suit with a T-shirt and a gold chain escorts his girlfriend, clad in Gucci's latest denim patch nightmare, toward Urbana.

"Didn't you used to dance at Runway 69?" the greaseball asks.

Lea inserts herself between them, gesticulating with the vodka she has already managed to get herself.

"Excuse me, Guido. But in case you didn't notice, these two happen to be with me. I mean, what the fuck is it with you guys? I thought this was supposed to be a lesbian party. *Lesbian?* Perhaps you'd like me to tear it off so you qualify."

Guido protests. "I have a right to be here, this is the United States, you know, you can't discriminate."

"I can't discriminate? Oh that's ripe, coming from a straight white man. What's the matter, baby doesn't feel like he belongs? Well, why don't you try a place that was set up just for you? Like the world!"

Lea downs her vodka and continues, "Thank you, lesbian chic! Oh, I wish we could just go back to the old days of feminism. Sure we didn't bathe, and all right, we had hair on our faces, but at least we didn't have to deal with stupid, sharkskin-suit-wearing, Iwanttowatchmygirlfriendfuckan-othergirl Neanderthals hitting on our dates."

Lea approaches the girl whom the increasingly annoyed sharkskin Guinea is with. She eyes her big hair up and down.

"And, Guido. Cute babe you got there. What a smart dresser. You know, I put my first patch on my jeans in grade four. I never knew I was pushing the trendsetting envelope. You know, there's a fine line between high fashion and science fiction . . . and speaking of New Jersey, what is that between your legs . . . could it be camel toe or are you just happy to see me?"

Lea lights another joint.

Xenia and Urbana begin to closely examine the Jersey chick's camel toe. Guido pulls off his sharkskin, signaling a "you want a piece of me" moment.

DeLaria is in full-swing alpha male, "my dick is bigger than yours," pissing-contest mode.

A drug dealer approaches and offers to sell the two cocaine. Lea screams, "Oh, yeah, offer me cocaine because I'm not hyper enough!"

Two large black men holding walkie-talkies overhear this remark and make their way toward the scene.

Xenia grabs Lea and Urbana and they dissolve.

"Fuck!" Lea screams, once inside another metaphysical plane. "Don't you ever stop me from having a fight." Xenia and Urbana blink in perplexity.

"But, Daddy Lea, large men with primitive two-way talking devices were approaching," Urbana says, then Xenia finishes, "Yes, they looked as if they would harm you."

"Well . . ." Lea shuffles her feet. "You could've at least waited for me to buy the coke."

Urbana nudges Xenia, who speaks. "There can be no doubt that you are our earthling guide, Lea DeLaria. However, you should be informed. We Venusians hold a keen interest in histrionics."

Urbana agrees. "Yes. We have compiled data on an event called . . . Pride? Will you take us there?"

Lea pulls at the flask she has removed from her back pocket. Then wipes her mouth. "Fuck Pride. Do I have to?"

Xenia and Urbana respond with a genuine offer. "We could pay you in Earth monetary units."

Lea notices the curve of Xenia's ass, then speaks. "Or we

could make a trade. Okay. Pride . . . only after that we go to the Forty-second Street Japanese baths, where they give full-release massages and think I'm a man."

Our group lands at a Pride Rally in Hartford, Connecticut. Xenia purchases an "Insurance Pride" T-shirt. Urbana notices a speaker onstage.

"What is she wearing, Daddy Lea?" Lea has just finished purchasing valerian root from the holistic earthy-crunchy remedies table.

Lea makes a yucky face and answers, "Fucking Hartford, I just want some downers and all I get is fucking roots." She looks at the stage. "That? That's a rainbow shirt."

Urbana covers her eyes. "It's burning my sprookets!" she screams. "There's nowhere to turn; it's everywhere!"

Xenia sees a Gay Pride flag and begins rolling on the ground, wailing, as if she's on fire.

"Help. Help. Make the rainbow stop!" they cry in pain.

Lea, realizing that the sight of rainbow is killing the Venusians, runs from table to table, desperately looking for two pairs of sunglasses. The only ones she finds have rainbow designs. When she finally comes across some Armani knockoffs, she runs back to her alien friends and puts them on their Munchian faces.

"I'm sorry, I'm sorry," Lea says, as she helps the two of them to their feet.

Urbana is dusting herself off, when Lea notices one of her breasts has popped from her bustier.

"Urbana, you might want to put that away."

"Is that necessary?" Urbana asks.

Lea thinks for a moment, and then replies, "No."

Xenia notices a banner over the stage. She begins to read aloud.

"Welcome to Hartford's Gay, Lesbian, Bisexual, Trans-gendered—"

"Bibbity, boppity, boo," DeLaria interrupts. "We used to just go to 'Gay Pride.' Now we march in the 'Gay, Lesbian, Bisexual, Transgendered, Transsexual . . .' By the time you're done saying it the fucking parade's over."

She spits the roots on the ground.

"This stuff is crap. Christ, some stressed-out insurance geek in this crowd has to have a Valium."

Xenia notices a lesbian couple with a baby and turns to Urbana.

"I thought you'd done all your homework on human reproduction before we got here. How'd they do that?"

Lea hears Xenia's comment and comes to Urbana's rescue.

"It's not her fault, she could have never known. None of us could have known. Babies have replaced softball gloves as the latest lesbian accessory. You know, I'm standing here right now listening to my biological clock tick." Lea pauses as two leather men walk by with their butts hanging out of their open-back chaps. "Fuck it. I'm watching my clock run out the fucking door and I'm happy. I'm ecstatic with my decision not to have kids."

Lea stomps her foot for emphasis, as Urbana jots down the gestures. Xenia repeats it, which starts the local Gay and Lesbian Rodeo Association in an impromptu line dance.

Several lesbians with children run over to join in the fun, surrounding Lea and the two Venusians.

"What is this?" Lea screams. "Gay Family Day? Love me. Love my cat. Love my dog. Love my kid. Love may make a family, but kids make a mess!

"And did someone pass a law recently saying lesbians have to adopt at least one Asian baby and name her Emma?

Is something wrong with Soon Lee or Lee Chen?" Lea pauses for breath support.

One lesbian mother yells, "Emma! Emma! Where are you?" at which point fifty little Asian girls run to her.

"It used to be," Lea continues, "you'd meet a girl, take her home, bang her brains out, and the next morning you give her coffee in a Styrofoam cup. Now every girl you meet wants you to marry her and be the father of her child."

"I thought you said you *wanted* to be called Daddy," Urbana points out.

Xenia is now thoroughly confused. "Marry?" she asks. "I am certain I read factoids relating your primitive society's nontolerance of earthlings with the same lativity to marry."

Lea raises a brow.

"Oh, you mean the Defense of Marriage Act? That's the law that makes it illegal for two gay men who've been together for twenty years to get married. But a straight man in Vegas can get drunk and marry a hooker in the Elvis Chapel."

Lea pulls out her flask and drains it.

Xenia and Urbana pull out a book and search frantically. "Vegas? Elvis? Hooker?"

Oblivious to their bafflement, Lea continues to spew. "I don't get this fucking marriage shit anyway. Everyone wants to get married. You know, when I came out, lesbians were feminists and feminists believed that monogamy was the exertion of male dominance over females. Therefore, in order to be a good feminist you had to fuck as many women as possible. And let me tell you, honey, I was a goooood feminist."

Lea begins to foam at the mouth. Xenia and Urbana look concerned, giving each other sideways glances.

"Let me ask you this, girls," Daddy Lea rants, not noticing her aliens' skeptical gazes. "Why the hell would anyone get married when they didn't have to? Let's face it: As queers, not having to get married is one of our perks. We don't get that goddamned many. We're ostracized by our families, our coworkers, our landlords, but at least we can fuck whoever we want!"

Xenia and Urbana take a few steps away from Lea, accidentally tripping into the "Everything Rainbow" tent. The close proximity of rainbow has an effect on them. Urbana begins to scratch, Xenia begins to twitch. Lea continues to continue.

"That is, if you can get some lesbian to fuck you! All they want to do is bitch about life, watch *Cagney & Lacey* reruns, and eat hummus! God, I could use a speedball right now. . . ."

Unbeknownst to Lea, Xenia and Urbana have jumped off midrave.

". . . Sometimes I wish I was fucking straight. And another thing . . . Where'd you go? Urbana? Xenia? Shit! Even Venusian lesbians are uptight."

Lea notices a twenty-year-old girl in a miniskirt and quickly scurries after her in an attempt to get a date.

Back on the ship, Xenia and Urbana return to their natural forms. Xenia speaks to Urbana.

"Well, smarty-tentacles, you really picked a great planet. Oh, yeah, they want to get laid, all right. It's just that they don't shut up long enough to do it."

Urbana is panicked. "What the hell are we going to tell Terpie?"

"Don't worry, Urbana honey, we'll just change the concept and get her to throw her Querns behind a package to Alpha Centauri. And I suppose if that doesn't work, we'll just have to have that wergway."

Urbana gets a glint in her eye. "You're a bad girl, Xenia. Now, come to Daddy."

They start to have sex. Xenia accidentally falls against the cloaking button, revealing the ship for all of Mir to see.

"Shto eto takoye," yells a cosmonaut, causing the international space community to come running to Mir's windows.

"It looks like some kind of ship. But what's that sticker on the bumper say?"

## RULE #4

Never . . . I repeat, NEVER,

point at anything beige

and call it "COOL."

# Bob

Bob is a bitch. He's not a total bitch, like a lot of really queeny fags. You know the type. They refer to everything: man, woman, dog, their boss, as "she." They watch the news, see a shot of Nelson Mandela.

"You go, girl," they say, trundling off to redecorate the dining room.

Bob is more conservative. But he can really go on a tear, which is why I don't want to be late to meet him for dinner. The "public place" rule does not apply to Bob.

An example. The public place: a Boston framing shop. A little-known fact about me is my affinity for art. I have been known to spend hours in the MOMA or the Tate and weeks at the Louvre. I spend a lot of time there. The fact that I am lost in these museums is irrelevant.

I collect gay and lesbian art. I'm reluctant to admit this. I fear I will be inundated with mailbags full of calendars depicting photographs of rocks that resemble vaginas. Lesbian artists see vaginas everywhere. It brings to mind those rampant Christians who see the face of Jesus beveled in the glass rear window of their double-wide trailer. I like vaginas as much as the next lesbian. However, I do try to refrain from searching for one in a piece of driftwood.

The gay male art scene is no better. Which is surprising; gay men are supposed to be "artistic." Is Tom of Finland art? Is he even from Finland? Does everyone in Finland have a dick the size of a redwood? If he's gay, why hasn't he changed his outfit in the last twenty-five years?

I collect good gay and lesbian art. I was in my

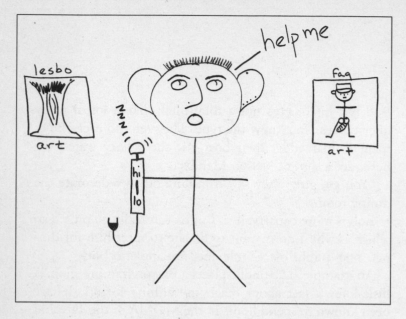

"photography period" and had just purchased three Lola Flash color negatives. I had enlisted Bob as my framing consultant.

We are in a tasteful framing shop on Newbury Street, agonizing over our options with the sole employee of the establishment. In walks . . . let's call her Mrs. Thurston Howell III. She seems to be in a dreadful hurry. Perhaps she is late for her three-hour tour.

"Can you please help me?" she asks Bob, without moving her jaw.

Bob, amused by the question, answers, "I'd love to help you, but I don't work here."

Unfettered, Mrs. Howell spins around faster than Lynda Carter morphing into Wonder Woman, and screeches at the saleswoman. "Well, then, you help me."

The saleswoman, believing that the customer is always

right, politely replies, "I'd be happy to help you, ma'am, once I'm through here."

We continue our business. After approximately two minutes, Lovey, who is clearly not used to being kept waiting, begins heaving, hemming, and hawing, like the radiator in a Trump tenement. Bob begins to tap.

*Exhale.*

Tap.

*Sigh.*

Tap. Tap.

*Ahem.*

Tap. Tap. Tap. Tap. Tap. Tap. Tap. Tap.

Oh, no. Bob is tapping his foot.

There are few sure things in life. The swallows return to Capistrano. Salmon swim upstream to mate. Seasons change. Bob tapping his foot means something interesting will occur.

Lovey, unaware of this natural phenomenon, crosses the street without looking. "Is this going to take much longer?"

The tapping stops. "Why? Are you having an art emergency?" Bob hisses.

Mrs. H, obviously alluding to Bob's effeminate demeanor, claws, "Does your mother like who you are?"

"My mother would be the first one to call you a cunt."

This is why I have no desire to be late for dinner. This, and the fact that Bob is my best friend. Bob and I have been best friends since before driver's licenses. If you take our age into consideration, Bob and I have been best friends longer than we haven't.

We were the type of high school friends who would drive around in a car for hours smoking weed and laughing at nothing. We were both gay but didn't bother to tell each other because we were positive that we were the only ones.

Remember, we grew up in a town in the Midwest that had been surrounded by an information shield since nineteen aught seven.

The first time I saw Bob he was wearing a short-sleeved checkered shirt buttoned all the way up to his neck. This was not a fashion statement . . . this was to cover his fat. He complemented his shirt with navy blue high-water polyester flairs rounded out with a white belt and shoes that matched. He carried every book for every class everywhere because "you never know when you'll get time to study!"

I, on the other hand, had long hair down to my ass that I rarely washed. I wore a dashiki with no bra and super-wide bell-bottom jeans that covered my eternally bare feet.

We invented the phrase "opposites attract."

Hard to believe that someone who dressed and acted like Bob in 1973 would get picked on, but it happened. Bob was tortured daily. As a Q.I.T. (Queen in Training), Bob was able to handle himself with a bitchy barb here and a sarcastic stab there. Of course, when he couldn't, I came in for the kill.

It's a tad easier to be gay in high school today than it was when I studied algebra.*

Today's teens have groups that lesbians can join. When I was sixteen, the only place in high school a lesbian was welcome was P.E.

Being "queer" was the worst thing that you could possibly be. Terrified that my ancient secret would be revealed, I

* I never actually studied in algebra class. But I had perfect attendance. Everyone but the teacher knew that was the time and place I sold LSD. Poor guy, I think he believed kids signed up for his class because they thought he was cool. Of course, after a hit of Orange Sunshine, everyone was cool. Peace, baby.

staunchly defended Bob when the other kids accused him of being a fag.

"He's my best friend, I'd know if he was queer."

It wasn't until the week before graduation that Bob decided enough was enough. We were in his red Granada, which he lovingly called Lucy. Suddenly, he pulled to the side of the road, lit up a joint, and took a big hit.

"Lea." He spoke while trying to keep the smoke in his lungs. "You have to stop telling people that I'm not a fag." He paused for dramatic effect, thereby gaining ten Q.I.T. points. "Because I am."

"You're kidding? So am I!" I squealed.

Bob laughed and passed me the joint in celebration. Then we scurried off to the nearest gay bar. He to dance disco, I to shoot pool.

How could I have not known his story? He named his car after Lucille Ball.

I quickly hop out of the cab as it pulls in front of our favorite restaurant, The King and Thai. I race in to find Bob tapping at the waiter.

Tap. Tap. Tap. Tap.

"Iced tea's not in season? Do you serve Coca-Cola?"

Tap. Tap. Tap. Tap.

"Good. Then get me a hot tea and serve it over the ice you were saving for that Coca-Cola. Lemon please. Thank you."

I bolt to the table, preparing myself to be "Bobbed" for being late. To my relief, Bob is not bothered. Instead he's absolutely giddy.

"Oh, I can't wait to tell you what happened at work today."

Goody, goody, goody, goody, goody. I love Bob work stories. Bob is employed at the Boston Symphony. Part of his job requires him to deal with symphony volunteers. The O.M.R.O.W.s (Old Moneyed Rich Old WASPs), as I like to call them, often refer to themselves by silly little pet names such as Mimsie, or Remy, or Bootsie. Such a volunteer once looked at Bob and said soberly, "Please, call me by my nickname, Pussy."

We order quickly and Bob launches into the story.

## bob's story

Bob, having finished his work for the day, makes his exit out the stage door and lights a cigarette. He notices a group of his coworkers in a heated discussion.

"What's up?" Bob asks.

Apparently, the artist liaison has accidentally forgotten to schedule a limousine pickup for Marilyn Horne, the evening's guest soloist. It is dangerously close to curtain and there is no time to organize appropriate transportation. The hotel limousine is unavailable, and you can't send a cab to pick up a woman in a forty-pound beaded gown.

Bob is about to lend his head to the "how the fuck are we going to get out of this one" production pool when it happens.

One tiny O.M.R.O.W. steps up to the plate.

"I'd be happy to pick up Ms. Horne in my car," she offers.

What could be more proper than a symphony patron personally escorting Ms. Horne to the theater in her Mercedes, or BMW, or maybe even her own chauffeur-driven limousine? Relieved, the production team agrees.

There they stand, congratulating themselves on the aversion of a near disaster, when the volunteer drives by tooting and waving from the inside of her lemon-yellow Volkswagen Beetle.

They all gawk in silence.

"Nice car," Bob says. "I think it's a '68."

No one but Bob is amused.

I believe that truly gifted people are also the most gracious. It's the insecure, untalented individuals who treat everyone with disdain and disrespect. Marilyn Horne is a truly gifted person.

The lemon-yellow Volkswagen returns, depositing Ms. Horne in full-beaded regalia. The swarm of production staff offering apologies and mea culpas is silenced by the diva's laughter.

"Oh, you owe me big, all right," she hoots, and begins her tale, which proves things are not always as bad as they appear. Sometimes, they're worse.

It seems the tiny O.M.R.O.W. met Marilyn Horne in the lobby of her hotel, then proceeded to lead her outside to the lemon-yellow chariot. "Well, I must say I'm a little disappointed," Ms. Horne justifiably reacted. "I thought there would at least be a limousine."

"You're disappointed," the tiny woman chirped, "I thought you were going to be Lena Horne."


Bob's iced tea arrives as we laugh at poor Marilyn's expense.

Tap. Tap. Tap.

"You forgot the lemon."

## RULE #5

Mistrust any individual who
does not close his or her eyes
when he or she kisses . . .
although how you will
know this without opening
yours is your problem.

# Gaelic Garlic

The Pope is on TV! You know, John Paul II, the traveling pope. He's been everywhere except the realm of reality. He's once again giving an interview. His holy thoughts are too numerous to repeat here, so I'll just give you my favorite. "It's all right to be a homosexual as long as you don't practice homosexuality." Isn't that an interesting observation? Especially when you consider it comes from a gentleman most often seen wearing a stunning white gown with gold lamé appliqué. When John Paul II, attired in his full regalia, drives about in the Pope Mobile, a vehicle which resembles a large bubble, it is a divine mystery that no one mistakes him for Glenda the Good Witch.

Whenever I see Dignity, the organization of gay/lesbian Catholics, at a Gay Pride event, I always wonder why they're not marching with the S/M contingent. Of course, my views are tainted by many years of Catholic school.

"Sister, what is a soul?" asks little seven-year-old me.

"Little girls who ask questions *go to hell* where their flesh will burn for all eternity and Satan devours their liver!" Irish nuns are sooo dramatic. I mean, even at the tender age of seven I found this hell scenario highly unlikely. Satan has his choice of any delicacy the world offers. Rack of lamb, Maine lobster, chateaubriand. Why eat prepubescent girl-liver?

I spent those long years with the Little Sister of the Pit Bull because my mother was forced into embracing Catholicism. I believed that's what it is called. In those days, in 1949, when the world was far too young to be growing old, Catholics could not marry outside the church. Hitler and Hiroshima, big bands and bebop, my mother and father.

My mother is the daughter of a bootlegger who delivered moonshine for Dutch Schultz, smart and smart-ass, wise at a time when good little wives weren't wise unless they hid it. My mother never thought to hide it. Her shrewishness is only surpassed by her Irishness, which I believe are one and the same.

My father is the son of Sicilian immigrants. Raised in Boston by the side of his family that is not "family," my father is the personification of the old adage, "There are two kinds of Italians; the kind you fuck and the kind you marry." My father is the latter, I am both.

Wops and Micks should never marry. Their children will only know how to fight and screw. The rest of life will be a huge blur. If Italians must marry outside their own, then let it be to Jews. Jews and Italians are the same people. Although our religion is perhaps less extreme, Jewish-light. Jews observe the Sabbath, Catholics celebrate Mass. Communion–Seder, Yom Kippur–Lent. Our likeness comes not from our faiths but rather the strictness of our cultures. Food and guilt run our lives. We Italians are just phlegmless Jews.

I was deprived of an Italian mother. I use the word "deprived" because we greaseball types are intensely proud of our heritage. I am, well, tainted with impure blood. It's like having syphilis without the fun part.

Once, years ago, I began an affair with a Canadian. She was very polite. She would say, "May I fist you?" and when she did, she'd extend her pinkie.

We began our tête-à-tête in an extremely small town at the edge of Cape Cod. We will call this town Provincetown because that's its name. Everyone figured out what was going on between us, because my Buick Skylark was parked in her drive overnight. The town's only other Buick Skylark belonged to a woman who had lost her legs to diabetes. She, therefore, was unable to drive. She could, however, wheel her motorized chair to the town's only main street and loudly protest anything from the stolen rights of the Native Americans to the planned construction of a Burger King. She could do this because she is a hippie.

So our clandestine liaison was anything but, and eventually the amorous Canuck was visited by her lover, the one she was cheating on with me. We will call the lover Maria Cannoli, although that is not her name, because you must comprehend how humungously Italian this woman is. She is the best bocci ball roller I have ever seen and can bake a seven-layer, three-meat, four-cheese lasagna that on a scale of one to ten rates a "beaver," beaver being slightly higher than ten. Meaning when you eat this luscious dish, it doesn't even make a pit stop at your stomach. It goes directly to your beaver. Cooking is one way we Italians get laid.

I know all of Maria's attributes because we are good friends. I toss the palina with her every Sunday, and afterward we go to her house and fight over the amount of garlic one should use in a meat gravy. She's Calabrese, and, like all the peasants, she saturates everything with too much oil and garlic.

When I was little, my father warned me to never date a Calabrese. "They screw sheep and beat their women," he said. I remember even then my prefeminist brain screaming, "See! See! He said 'screw sheep' before 'beat women.' All men suck." But I digress.

Right now you are thinking that I am an asshole. I must

be to carry on with a good friend's lover, but hey, it's hard being a dyke. As a people, we lean toward the incestuous. There are actually only six lesbians. We do it with mirrors. My ex goes out with her ex, who's doing it with her current, who used to be my ex's current ex . . . you see what I mean. Now add to this the small-town syndrome, in which people become a pass-around pack and well, you could understand how I might find myself in bed with a good friend's wife. That and when it comes to sex, I'm an asshole. But I have an excuse. I'm Italian.

Okay, Maria visits her Canadian soon-to-be-ex, my current-future-ex, in order to present her with the gossip that has ripped through town with the speed of Godzilla eating Asians.

"Is it true?" Maria asks bluntly.

Uh-oh. Trouble. See, I'm an American, I shudder to say. As a lesbian, I feel about as American as the banjo boy in *Deliverance*. However, I must admit certain aspects of Americana do rub off on me. Frankly I'd be happier if Sigourney Weaver would rub off on me, but who wouldn't. In the eyes of the world, American = loud. American = obnoxious. American = confrontational. This is ironic, as most Americans feel precisely that way about Italian-Americans, especially Americans fucking Italian-Americans.

So, as you can imagine, spurned Maria "Is it true?" Cannoli was feeling particularly loud, obnoxious, and confrontational. Big mistake. You see, Maria forgets the person she is speaking to is not American. She believes she is dealing with someone like, well, me. I would deal with this scenario like any red-blooded American raised by Ward and June and Eddie Haskell. Lie. Not just any old lie, but bold, looking-directly-in-your-face-with-the-smell-of-pussy-juice-on-my-chin lie.

"Oh, sweetie, of course it's not true. When are you going to stop giving credence to town rumor and innuendo? My God! You know how mean-spirited these small-town bitches can . . . what's that on my chin? Oh, I was eating a tuna sandwich. Yeah, lots of mayo. Now, sugar, look, you know you've got to rise above this sort of old woman gossi—that? That's No-Legs-Sheila's car. She dropped it by this morning. Baby, you won't believe this, but she actually grew legs. I think she used some kind of bizarre Dolly cloning cocktail mixed with Rogaine by-product. She wants me to change the oil."

That sort of lie, and I believe Maria expected this, even wanted this, but my angry guineawopdagogreaseball friend forgets she is dealing with a Canadian, as in from Canada, land of nice. Confrontation will not do. Why, the mere spelling of the word is enough to send anyone born and raised north of the border screaming from the building, "Get out of the house, he's on the extension!"

The Canadian, whom we will call Lesley, using the English spelling because she is precisely that sort of Canadian, when confronted with confrontation did what any red-blooded Canuck would do in any situation. She apologized.

"I'm sorry," our polite friend whispered, as it is hard for Canadians to speak out loud in public. "It's true."

I wish I could say I knew what happened next because of town gossip or legend, but the sad truth is I was in the next room, behind closed doors, cowering under the bed like a grocery delivery boy in a bad French farce. It would have been worth it if instead of Lesley it had been Catherine Deneuve.

Although I'm a little pissed at Catherine. Recently she sued a small lesbian magazine because they had the audacity to name their little tome *Deneuve*. When it was settled out of court with a stipulation that the rag must change its name, I suggested they call it *Stupid Homophobic Blond Frog Bitch*. Our Catherine insists her battle had nothing to do with homophobia, commerce being the motive. She had just put out her new cologne, also entitled *Deneuve*, and felt people might confuse the magazine for the perfume. Like I could go shopping for a *Playboy* and come home with a bottle of Chloe. But I digress.

So I'm under the bed and I actually hear her tell the truth.

"Are you nuts?" both Maria and I say in perfect unison, although not for the same reasons. I said it out of shock, wondering whether if the need arose I could get my ass through the Cape Cod saltbox window, knowing if I got stuck this would turn from a French farce into the Three Stooges. Maria said, "Are you nuts?" in order to launch into a recitation of my many faults and evils, thereby belittling me and making herself the better of us two. There was a slight wrinkle. Whatever my problems were, Maria could top them with dominatrix ability. I knew it. Lesley knew it. And worst of all, Maria knew it. So all she could say was "Are you nuts?" and then there was this long pause that eventually turned into a pregnant pause, which finally birthed a notion. What horrible and fiendish quality did I possess that could be the ruination of all concerned?

"You know, Lesley," Maria emphatically declared, "Lea is not a full Italian." She then turned and stomped off wearing a smug "I have revealed the secret," Liz Smith grin.

Maria forgot one tiny detail, however: "full Italian" blood is only important to the Mafia and finicky Venetian vampires. So when I had finally removed myself from under the rather tight squeeze of the bed and made it into the

living room, I found Lesley laughing . . . not like a hyena—
she is, after all, Canadian—but more like an owl.

"HOOT . . . you're only half Italian . . . HOOT . . .
Who knew! . . . HOOT! . . . You don't fuck like a half
Italian."

"I'll show you how much I fuck like an Italian," I
growled, and using all the subtlety of an Italian I pushed
Lesley down on the rug and climbed on top, holding her
arms above her head so that she could not move. Then, using my best Bronx accent, I seduced, "Let's do it right here
on the Oriental."

Her response was one word.

"PIG."

What happened next? That's none of your business, a
sentiment that comes from my Irish half.

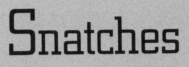

# Snatches

When writing a book, it is not uncommon to find yourself editing out little sections and stories. These sections and stories are deemed useless to the cute little essay from which they have departed.

Well, I just could not live without them . . . which, by the way, is exactly how I feel about my subscription to *Barely Legal* . . . so here they are.

# Quotes

"Problems. I don't have problems. Problems are for poor people."
—SHANNEN DOHERTY, *Interview in* TV GUIDE.

"Every apple has to have a peeling."
—CALISTA FLOCKHART, *Trying to sing "There's No Business Like Show Business" to open the 1999 Tony Awards ceremony.*

"Oh, my coccyx."
—GWYNETH PALTROW, *When asked to ad-lib crowd noise during* AS YOU LIKE IT *rehearsals.*

"Young man. Do you know this is the ladies' room?"
—*Unknown blue-haired bitch speaking to me in the bathroom at the Shubert Theater, where I was performing a benefit.*

"He takes this very personally . . . I mean, it's like a personal thing with him. I don't know why he takes it so personal."
—O. J. SIMPSON, *In a radio interview, referring to Ron Goldman's father.*

"And now, ladies and gentlemen, Duke Ellington's 'Take a Train.'"
—LAWRENCE WELK, *On his show.*

"There is this one cat and he is very, very sad. So the other cats try to cheer him up by singing and dancing.

P.S. It doesn't work. So they put him in a tire and blow him through a hole in the roof."
—A MATINEE LADY, *Explaining the story of* CATS *to another matinee lady.*

"I'd like to take this opportunity to give Lea DeLaria a great big kiss."
—BERNADETTE PETERS, *In her speech at the Drama League Luncheon . . . I may never recover.*

"Call me Miss Birdseye, but this show is frozen."
—ETHEL MERMAN, *Final dress,* GYPSY.

"If you think of it, it's a bit. If I think of it, it's a gag."
—GEORGE WOLFE, ON THE TOWN *rehearsals.*

"When a boy and a girl touch dance there should be enough room between them to throw a cat."
—SISTER MELISSA, *My eighth-grade nun, during a sex education lecture.*

# Beside Myself

## beside myself

Recently a group of fags . . . what would you call a group of fags? Recently a ram of fags took me out for an evening of fun. Frankly, I'm very easy to please around such things. An evening of fun for me consists of my fist, Alyssa Milano, and a quart of Crisco. Alas, the ram had other ideas.

We met at a neighborhood place, a small watering hole on the Upper West Side, or UpWe, as I like to call it.

If you live in the area you may have seen this dive. There is a water faucet logo on the front door. Emblazoned around the faucet are the words "The Water Works."

It's an odd name for a gay bar, almost too sweet. When one has been involved in the ghetto as long as I, one gets used to seeing gay bars named Moby Dick or Cock-a-

Doodle-Doo. The only reason I can determine for naming a gay place The Water Works is if it is a piss club.

The Works, as the boys who frequent the place for beer-blast Sundays lovingly call it, is not a piss club, except perhaps on beer-blast Sundays. No. The Works is a video bar. Had I known this I would have avoided the place like Martha Stewart's anus.

I hate video bars, especially gay video bars. To my taste the only establishment worse than a video bar is a piano bar. I hate, loathe, and despise piano bars. Is there anything more annoying than some queen who can't make it on Broadway mixing a Cosmopolitan while singing *Pippin*?

### annoying singing bartender:
Do you want a lime in that?

### me:
yes

### annoying singing bartender:
Everything has its season
Everything has its time
Show me a—

### me:
SHUT UP SHUT UP SHUT UP!!!

I hate gay video bars for two reasons.

### two reasons lea hates gay video bars

### 1. The videos

### 2. The videos

Every time a human enters a gay video bar, said human encounters on said video screen a gay porn video. Sex, I believe, is the one thing men need no reminding of.

### things men need reminding of

1. Rotate their tires

2. Fill out their tax return

### 3. PUT DOWN THE TOILET SEAT

4. Not to hooch at nun's hooters

5. Look both ways before stepping off a curb

6. Not to download anything from Germany with the words "scheisse" and "essen" in the title

Sex is something men always seem to have a grip on . . . so to speak, and since gay men are two men having sex . . . well . . . need I write more?

I mean, let's face it, fagallas, you boys don't even make it into the bar.

## the first date

**FIRST FAGALLA**
Hi.

**SECOND FAGALLA**
Hi.

**FIRST FAGALLA**
Wanna fuck in the bushes?

**SECOND FAGALLA**
Sure.

Which brings me to the companion joke, which I wrote for the classic "What does a lesbian bring on a second date" joke I did in 1989.

**Q. What does a gay man bring on a second date?**
**A. What second date?**

The second thing I hate about gay video bars is the other videos. You, gentle reader, may be unaware of this, but I have been an openly gay performer since 1982, having starred with my mother and father on the Orpheum Circuit when I was four.

In that amount of time, I have done a lot of television. Not counting my guest appearances on shows like *Friends*, where I convincingly portrayed a lesbian inappropriately hitting on a straight woman (not that I have any experience to help with that character), or *The First Wives Club*, where I portrayed a lesbian inappropriately hitting on a straight woman, or *Saved by the Bell*, where I portrayed a lesbian . . . wait a minute, I didn't play a lesbian inappropriately hitting on a straight girl on *Saved by the Bell*. I think that was a beautiful dream I had once.

I have a vast amount of television screen time devoted solely to "openly gay" material, possibly more screen time than any other openly gay performer . . . with the possible exception of Julia Child, who is one badass motherfucker.*

Having all this "openly gay" screen time—dare I call it "wide-openly gay" air time, for when I perform, that is

---

* Apparently, using the phrase "one badass motherfucker" does not quell the fears of my publisher's lawyer. I must state to you as if you are an idiot that I am merely joking when I refer to Julia Child as a lesbian. She could never be a lesbian; she cooks with red meat.

more to the point—it is only natural that gay video-type joints have a "Lea DeLaria Stockpile-o-Shit."

Every time I enter a gay video beerhaus, without fail at the shank of the evening, when everyone's really digging the scene, just as my E kicks in, the music stops. I look up to see me. I am surrounded by me on every goddamn video monitor in the place, little Lea images floating around truly walking on my cloud, man.

On this particular night my ram of fags decides to take me out for an evening of fun at the neighborhood gay video bar, The Works.

We are in there for about two hours enjoying ourselves. It is the shank of the evening. Everyone is really digging the scene. My E kicks in. Suddenly the music stops.

"Fuck," I think, wishing I had done Special K or even heroin, because then I would be unconscious.

I look up and yes . . . out comes little Lea on every monitor in the place.

I am unsure what show it is. I truly don't care. I just want to play with my friends. I just want to be left alone. I just want a little understanding . . . *ein bisschen Verstehen.* So I put my head down on the bar and exclaim aloud, "Oh, no!"

The little gay boy on the next bar stool notices my reaction and assumes, making an ass only of himself. He nudges me, and as I look up he says, "Oh, I know just how you feel. I hate that woman, too."

# Lists

## things you never hear an agent say

1. You don't weigh enough to play this role.

2. Why, I just happen to have a puppeteer in my office right now.

## state license plate slogans

1. We inbreed here

2. Alli alli unsenfreed

3. Land of unwashed feet

4. The unconscious state

## reasons to despise mormons

1. They think they're better than you.

2. The Book of Mormon

3. They live in Utah.

4. They don't drink coffee.

5. They'll believe anything.

## magazines we can do without

1. *Trance.* The magazine for people who get hypnotized.

2. *Tattoo.* Is this necessary?

3. *Tranz.* The magazine for people who get sex-changed.

4. *Troll.* The magazine for boyz who like old bearded guys.

and that just covers the T's.

## people you'd only fuck if you got stuck with them on a desert isle

1. Gilligan

2. Skipper

3. The Professor

4. Mr. Howell

5. Al Gore

## why lesbians whine

1. Because they can.

2. Who's going to stop them?

3. They all get their periods at the same time.

4. They don't eat meat.

# Wake Up, I'm Fat! ... But Not As Fat As Camryn Manheim.*

* Actually, there is no essay. I just like the title.

# The Sartorial Question

Once upon a time it was very simple to dress for dykecess. All one needed were ten pairs of Doc Martens boots (black), ten pairs of baggy jeans (black), ten turtleneck sweaters (black), and one motorcycle jacket (black, or pink if you like people to mock you). This attire works if you are dancing in the local lesbian establishment or just planning to burglarize it.

The Urban Trendy Poser Dyke Look, or U.T.P.D.L., began at the earlier part of the nineties, and may I state here and now that it was a vast improvement over the crunchy granola sister woman look, or C.G.S.♀.L., which was all *too* prevalent in lesbian fashion circles of the seventies and eighties.

## <u>C.G.S.♀.L.</u>

### 1. Lavender drawstring pants

### 2. Rainbow suspenders

### 3. Purple T-shirt exclaiming a political slogan

### 4. Accessorize with a tub of hummus

Actually, the C.G.S.♀.L. can still be seen today in San Francisco; Madison, Wisconsin; Northampton, Massachusetts; and various areas of New Mexico, although the girls thusly robed in New Mexico are less likely to be lesbians and more likely to be hippies who smoked a tad too much reefer, lost their short-term memory, and misplaced Taos.

Gone are the days of dress ease, for alas, the U.T.P.D.L. has run its course and now the world looks at women loving women in a whole new fashion-oriented way.

## lesbian chic

Yes. Somehow it happened. Although how a group that collectively drinks enough lite beer to burp "The Star Spangled Banner" in perfect, gaseous, three-part harmony can become "chic" is beyond me.

INT:　Camera fades in on a foggy haze of a bedroom. Two smoky figures lie in bed. As the camera pulls focus we see that they are hugely fat and wearing flannel pajamas.

close-up:　The first woman looks directly into the camera.

**WOMAN ONE**
I am fat and I am watching *Xena*.

INT:　Woman Two turns on her side. We see she is holding a hockey stick.

INT:　Two cats run across the bed.

**WOMAN TWO (calling to cats)**
Gertrude. Alice.

INT:　One cat knocks over a mug of chai tea.

INT:　The two women gaze deeply into each other's eyes.

**WOMAN ONE AND TWO (unison)**
I am fat and I am watching *Xena*.

INT:    Camera pulls out of focus as the two put their heads together.

**v.o. (female)**

Fallopian Tube.    The new fragrance from Calvin Klein.

fade out as:    A sea gull calls.

The "chic" journey of my people started in 1992 and has continued to the present day, which means the lesbian as a significant fashion must is almost as durable as the little black dress. Yet even with the healthy run we have endured, some people are still unsure as to how to make the proper lesbian sartorial statement.*

And so it is that I have taken it upon myself to help you, gentle reader, become more efficient and effective with the correct use of the lesbian as a fashion statement.

As in all arenas of haute couture, there are important details to consider.

## <u>haute couture considerations</u>

### 1. Setting

### 2. Function

### 3. Statement

Let us examine these in order.

---

* Recently, the woman I am dating and I were discussing auditions. She asked a question, to which I replied, "Do you mean your sartorial statement?" Her brow ruffled. "No," she emphatically exclaimed, "I mean my clothes."

## setting

In order to choose the proper lesbian, one must first know where one is going. For example, one should never arrive at the Westchester Country Club wearing Fran Lebowitz, unless of course you are ready to do a "Gentleman's Agreement" sort of battle at the door. Although, if such a fight is in the plan, it is fortuitous that you are wearing a lesbian, as being argumentative is a lesbian prerequisite. Argumentativeness is on the lesbian prerequisite list under "Having a Wicked Tabouli Recipe," and on top of "Having Incredible Sex with Lea DeLaria."

## function

Having now determined "where" you are excursing, it is a good idea to consider "why" or "what for." Is this a formal occasion? If so, showing up accessorized by Janet Reno could be a mistake. The conversation would be exquisite; however, the atmosphere would be horrifically changed. Better to use Cherry Jones, or for that extra-special occasion, Lauren Hutton, who matches black tie beautifully. . . . Let's face it, Lauren Hutton could match a black hole beautifully.*

## statement

Or "What am I trying to say about me?" Am I:

**whimsical—Linda Hunt
practical—Gina Gershon**

---

* Or my hole beautifully. My publisher's lawyer wants me to explain that I have no idea whether or not Lauren Hutton is gay. I merely hope she is.

**funky—Sandra Bernhard**
**fun—Me'Shell NdegéOcello**
**plain—Chastity Bono**

All right. Gina Gershon isn't actually a true lesbian. She is an honoree. It's very simple to become an honoree. One must first be female, then one must do one of two things.

### two things one must do to become a true lesbian honoree

1. Act a lesbian role more than once

2. Be seen talking to a lesbian

Now that you have some idea of how one should choose the sapphic style that best suits oneself, let's put it to the test in some moot yet interesting situations:

## interesting situation one

You have been invited to weekend with your boss and his wife at their place in the Hamptons.

### pick one

a) Janice Ian

b) Roseanne's sister

c) The drummer from Luscious Jackson

d) All of the above

e) None of the above

Answer: **e.** You could never impress any boss who owns a place in the Hamptons and actually uses the word "weekend" as a verb.

## interesting situation two

Your ex-boyfriend is marrying your ex–best friend. You haven't spoken to either of them since you walked in on them having sex in the apartment you and he shared over two years ago. Yet you have received a peace offering in the form of an invitation.

### pick one

a) Ellen DeGeneres

b) Anne Heche

c) Marilyn Manson*

d) All of the above

e) None of the above

Answer: **c.** Must I explain this?

## interesting situation three

Ted Kennedy has invited you to the Hyannis compound for some sailing, a bite to eat, and a rousing game of touch football.

---

* Honoree, kids. Saw her talking to the forward of the New York Liberty . . . What do you mean she's a he?

## pick one

a) The girls from The Murmers

b) Missy Giove

c) The president of the Gay and Lesbian Republican Club

d) All of the above

e) None of the above

Answer: this one's a tad tougher than the others. The correct answer is **c.** You see, she and Ted would spend so much energy arguing policy that he wouldn't have time to mentally picture her naked with another woman, thereby embarrassing himself by excusing himself to dash off and attend to his little soldier in Rose's old bedroom. One should always consider one's host.

Well, it seems you have the gist of it and I must dash, as I've been invited to a Mets game. I have just enough time to throw on the center of the U.S.A.'s Women's Soccer Team.* Ta.

---

* Okay, I don't know if she is a lesbian; however, she is the center of a women's soccer team so I'm certain she's been seen talking to one.

## RULE #6

It's okay to fuck *anyone* . . .

as long as you've

seen them dance.

# Somewhere over the Sixth-Floor Walk-up

I am the world's most rabid Judy Garland fan. Now I will pause and wait for the roars of contempt from the faggot contingent to die down. Boys, I know you believe that you invented Judy, but the sad truth is she was a star before she was ever aware of your existence.

Oh, yes, and to you other gentlemen who insist on donning your favorite Garland gown and singing "clang, clang, clang went the trolley," would you please get your *own* life. Judy's was hard enough.

I was once asked to participate in a "Judy Garland Contest." The object, as I understood it, was for each man to make himself up like Judy, dress like Judy, and lip-synch to one of Judy's recordings. Yet I was to judge them on "originality." Need I say more?

I loved Judy from the start. I grew up in the sort of family that believed in togetherness—the family that plays together . . . , which usually manifested in my uncle showing up in my bedroom at three A.M. Wearing my mother's bra.*

Sometimes, however, it meant the entire unit watching television. Usually we got through the evenings without a hitch. We all had similar taste. Thursday *Star Trek*, Friday *Dragnet* and *Perry Mason*, Saturday was reserved for Jackie Gleason and later my idol Carol Burnett.

---

* Okay, my uncle never molested me or anyone else that I know of with the possible exception of my aunt, who, I believe, welcomed it. However I would be happy if he molested my publisher's lawyer, if only to get him off my ass.

When looking at this rather normal lineup, one could assume Sunday equaled *Bonanza*, and in our house sometimes it did, except on those Sundays when my parents finally got tired of my "incessant" "Why can't we watch Judy? Why can't we watch Judy? Why can't we watch Judy, WHY CAN'T WE WATCH JUDY?"

My love affair with Judy became personal when she helped me find an apartment. It was 1986 and I had just moved to New York from San Francisco, after the breakup of a five-year relationship. She got the West Coast in the divorce.

I was young and naïve. I believed it would be simple to locate affordable housing in New York. I am no longer this young. That is why I demanded an apartment rather than a relocation fee when I came to New York for *On the Town*. I know it is easier to get a lead on Broadway than it is to find an apartment in Manhattan.

I had been searching for months and was growing rather weary of sleeping on friends' couches, on friends' floors, and on friends.

One evening I am reading *The Village Voice* and having a beer in The Old Duchess. You remember The Old Duchess, don't you, girls? At one time it was NYC's only dyke bar, so everyone had to go there. In The Duchess it was not unusual to see fat, working-class Puerto Rican butches hitting on big-haired Long Island heiresses. I once witnessed one such encounter. The butch eyed the heiress up and down. She then calmly strolled over, hitched her thumbs in her belt loops, and spoke. "Yo, I like da way youse dress."

On this particular evening The Duchess is quiet. I am miserable in my beer. I am miserable because I am staying with a friend who really, really likes me. I mean she *really likes* me, and I know if I continue to stay with her I will sooner or later have to have sex with her. I do not want to have sex with her. We are friends. One should not have sex with one's friends, it will ruin the relationship. Besides, she is coyote ugly.

Suddenly I see it, the perfect ad.

### the perfect ad

**two gay men sking 3rd.**
**Own room. $200. First and last**
**555–3481**

As I mentioned, I was young and naïve so I believe that "sking 3rd" meant a third "person."

I jump from the barstool, call the number, and receive the directions. Two subway trains and six flights of stairs later I am knocking on what I hope will be my new front door.

"Just a minute," the somewhat mincing voice inside demurs, as he unlocks what sounds like approximately nine different bolts. "You can't be too careful in this . . ."

His lisp is stunned into silence. Then he squeals, "Girl! You're a REAL GIRL!"

There is no way to describe what is happening in my brain at this moment. However, since this is an essay, and that is precisely what I am supposed to do, I will try.

My ex's face is floating around taunting and laughing—this is cut with scenes of me roaming the streets of New York giving hand jobs for a room. Back to my ex's face, which morphs into my coyote-ugly friend and I'm . . . WHAT? GOING WHAT DIRECTION ON HER . . . Then, of course, there's the six flights I just walked up.

In a split second I know what I must do. I must convince

this man that inside my big bulldyke body beats the heart of a vicious queen.

I sing show tunes. I imitate Bette Davis. I quote every line that I know from *Auntie Mame*.

". . . And I stepped on the Ping-Pong ball."

He is laughing. It is working. I am cheekbones, cheekbones, cheekbones.

Then disaster strikes.

"You know, Bill," I say to Bill, for Bill is his name, "I am the world's most rabid Judy Garland fan."

"You are not," Bill replies.

"I am to," I counter.

"Are not."

"Am to."

"Are not."

"Am to."

"Are not."

"You can have Liza."

Apparently Bill is unimpressed by my Liza joke. He storms from the living room.

"What have you done?" I scream in my head. "You stupid dyke bitch, you are arguing about Judy Garland with a faggot, a FAGGOT. JUDY FAGGOT, FAGGOT JUDY, are you INSANE!!! Have you lost what's left of your lesbian sanity? He's a FAG!"

I and the little voice in my head are certain I have just lost this apartment. Then, without warning, Bill returns. He is, of course, wearing a new ensemble, having had enough time to fume and then change.

"You may have the room," he says, as he sits and crosses his legs, making certain I will notice the rhinestone trim on his ball gown, "if you answer one question correctly."

I tremble with anticipation. He uses the pause beautifully and to full effect, placing his hand on his crossed knee to reveal the matching ring.

"What is the last song on side one of *Judy at Carnegie Hall*?"

Now it is my turn. I dim the track lights, for this is a gay man's apartment in 1986, so of course there is track lighting and of course they are on a dimmer. I stand next to—what else—the fern, and I start to sing.

"Alone. Together."

"Above the crowd."

He joins me. "We're not too proud."

We finish the number and he gives me the key.


I lived with Bill for three years. He was a slob. Odd for a gay. Odd for a Jew. Well, Bill was always a misnomer. I use the past tense, because Bill has passed.

Perhaps it's maudlin, but I do like to think that somewhere, out there, over the sixth-floor walk-up, Bill and Judy are having a few laughs at my expense.

Maybe even singing, "In my high-starched collar and my high-topped shoes, and my hair piled high upon my head."

## RULE #7

Do not look in the mirror

and say, "I love you."

The mirror is most

likely to reply,

"Couldn't we just be friends?"

# Slippery When Wet, Even More Dangerous When Dry

You guessed it, I'm talking about women. If there's a statement that's more appropriate as applied to women, I don't know what it is. Because the fact is, once the slube dries up, the trouble begins.

Oh, it's all fine and good in the heat of passion, in those first six months when you can't believe that anyone else on the planet ever graced your face. "No, really, she really is the one. She's so smart, she's so funny, she's so talented . . ." She's soooo history.

And now that she is history, the real pain in the ass begins, the degrees of which vary with the particular type of ex you have. There are many varying degrees of exes, so I've devised a test to establish your own personal ex pain-in-the-ass quotient. E.P.A.Q. Take the test, add up your score, and that's how many years of misery you can expect from the bitch you once called Muffin.

Before we get started, though, I'm going to have to dispel a few myths.

**Myth Number One:** *It's Okay to Be Best Friends with Your Ex.*

It's not okay. It's not only not okay, it's probably a sign of some kind of pathology.

She's your ex. She can't be your best friend. If she were your best friend, you'd want to fuck her. A person always wants to fuck his or her best friend, that's half the draw of having them around. If you've already fucked, they are immediately disqualified from holding the title of "best friend." Plus, your current girlfriend will insist that you tell her that *she's* your best friend. If you're going to keep your ex on as a best friend you might as well just keep fucking her and stay in the relationship, or you can have the first date of your next relationship at the therapist's office.

## Myth Number Two: *If You Ignore Her, She'll Go Away.*

Buzzzzzz. Thank you for playing the game. In fact, nothing could be further from the truth. You can't just say, "Fuck her." You already did, and therein lies the problem.

Exes are like boils. You can ignore one all you want, but the fact is that eventually—for example, when it's overtaken your entire left buttock—you're going to have to lance it.

Don't treat your ex like that boil. We all know what happens when you finally do lance: You're left to deal with the nasty ooze. Frankly, it's not that pretty.

Worse yet, when they are not properly handled, boils explode on their own. Meaning, she's out there. You know it. She knows it. She knows you know it. Attend to it. Even if it's just faking a pleasant hello. You faked loving her for the last three years of your relationship. You can fake hello.

## Myth Number Three: *You Can Trust a Person to Hold Your Confidence.*

I should qualify here. Of course you can trust a person to hold your confidence. As long as it doesn't have to do with your ex! Anything you say about your ex to anyone, anywhere, at any time, can be used against you in a court of law. Especially if one is dealing with lesbians.

Dare I say that? Lesbians? Judgmental? You bet your ass

I can say it. I can even say it three times fast. Judgmental lezzies, judgmental lezzies, judgmental lezzies. Let's face it. Half the time, dykes are just looking to take a side. Since the ERA fizzled, we've had nothing.

Go ahead. Try to get your side of the story out. Your words will end up so twisted you'll think you invented the pretzel. I don't care how much you think you can trust her. Unless the person you're talking to is your best friend from grade two who happens to be straight and hasn't a clue who your ex is, save it for your journal.

**Myth Number Four:** *She'll Never Tell Anyone All the Stuff You Told Her in Bed.*

Tell me you didn't. Because not only will she tell everyone the stuff you told her in bed, she'll tell everyone the stuff you *DID* in bed. Especially if she thinks it will somehow damage your reputation, such as, say, at your bowling league. Get over this one quickly. The fact is, the asshole she's with now is not only wearing your old jeans, she knows what you did in them.

**Myth Number Five:** *I'm Not Leaving You for* _____ *(fill in the blank). Besides, she's (pick one):*

a. In a relationship.

b. Straight.

c. Celibate.

d. Just needing a place to stay until:

**(pick one again)**

1. She can get away from her abusive boyfriend.

2. She gets her own place.

3. It doesn't matter what I say, because moving this woman into our home is so ridiculous that I might as well just hit you on the head with her vulva.

Let me get my bullhorn out for this one:

She'll say she hasn't, but deep down you know she already has. You can ignore the obvious. However, you can't ignore that itch you developed since they started hanging out. Especially since you know you haven't been with anyone else. Sorry, you don't get that from a toilet seat. Pick up the phone, call your lawyer, your mover, and your doctor, not necessarily in that order.

Now, if you've managed to move through these myths

without wondering if I wasn't in fact also involved with your ex, you're ready to take the test. Got your pencil? Okay, then, ready? Here you go.

## e.p.a.q. test

**1. Your ex calls your house and hangs up, first being careful to either block identification of her call or call from her cell phone so you have no idea who it is:**

    a. Every day. (5 points)
    b. Every other day. (3 points)
    c. Once, in a weak moment. (1 point)
    d. Never. (0 points)

**2. Your ex calls your supervisor at work and hangs up, first being careful to either call from her home or her work so that her phone number shows up on your supervisor's caller ID for you to see, causing enormous amounts of stress and anxiety:**

    a. Every fucking day. (5 points)
    b. Every other day. (3 points)
    c. Once, when she had to do business with your company, but at the last minute realized that it would probably be better if she talked to someone else in the company. (1 point)
    d. Never. (0 points)

**3. Your ex drives by your new residence:**

    a. Every day, every hour on the hour. (5 points)
    b. Every other day. (3 points)

c. Once, when she took a wrong turn. (1 point)

d. Never. (0 points)

## 4. Your ex wreaks havoc with your travel plans by canceling your plane, car, or hotel reservations:

a. Always. It's her vocation. She's quit her job and dedicated her life to it. (5 points)

b. Only plane reservations. (3 points)

c. Only once, when without knowing the entire reservation would be lost, she canceled her part of a two-week vacation you purchased together before the breakup. (1 point)

d. Never. (0 points)

## 5. Your ex mispronounces your new girlfriend's name, with disdain dripping from her fanglike teeth:

a. Every stinking time the two of you run into her. (5 points)

b. Every third time the two of you run into her. (3 points)

c. Once, but she didn't realize your girlfriend's name had an accent on the first "e," and apologized immediately. (1 point)

d. Never. (0 points)

## 6. Your ex still corresponds with your family:

a. Every birthday, holiday, or funeral, even if it's just the funeral of a third cousin twice removed. (5 points)

b. Every holiday. (3 points)

c. Only to send an appropriate sympathy card. (1 point)

d. Never. (0 points)

## 7. Your ex shows up where she knows you'll be at the exact time she knows you'll be there and then pretends that she's either entirely shocked to see you or that you're

somehow an asshole for being there even though it's your parent's house and it's your birthday:

a. Every single motherfucking time. (5 points)
b. Just when she knows it will have the most impact. (3 points)
c. Once, when your mom accidentally sent her an invite and she felt obligated to go because, well, she always liked your mom. (1 point)
d. Never. (0 points)

**8. Your ex fills your e-mail with computer viruses that cause your computer to turn on itself and eat every last piece of data including your journal, which your ex knows you keep and use as a way to heal yourself in troubled times and without which you would probably lose your mind:**

a. Shit yes. She's even got a dedicated modem line, just for the very purpose of redialing and sending you spam/virus-ridden e-mail twenty-four hours a day, seven days a week. (5 points)
b. Only when she logs on. (3 points)
c. Once, by accident, when she was forwarding you an uplifting Audre Lorde poem she found on a Web site that happened to be corrupt and the virus attached itself to the file. (1 point)
d. Never. (0 points)

**9. Your ex fakes illness, or a family tragedy, or the illness of a once–co-owned pet:**

a. So often that your friends are starting to call her the Baroness Munchausen. (5 points)

b. A few times, when her aunt really did have cancer, but it was only a small melanoma on her chin. (3 points)
c. Once, but she genuinely thought the dog went missing, only to find him snuggled up in the basement on a pile of your old clothes. (1 point)
d. Never. (0 points)

**10. Your ex keeps all your mail, refusing to forward any of it:**

a. You bet your ass. Your credit has become so bad you've had to fake a new Social Security number just to make a purchase at Sears. (5 points)
b. She sends you the stuff from Ed McMahon. (3 points)
c. Only once. It was addressed to both of you and only after two weeks did she realize it was your cellular phone bill, since you got the phone in the divorce. (1 point)
d. Never. (0 points)

## the rating

### 40–50 points = P.E.G.

Psycho Ex-Girlfriend. She's all over your shit, honey. She sees you when you're sleeping, she knows when you're awake, she knows if you've been bad or good . . . Sorry, I broke into song. The reality on this one is that you're going to need a restraining order, the white trash badge of courage. Otherwise, you're doomed to a life of getting P.E.G.-ed all over the place. Yipes! Look out, here she comes now.

## 20–39 points = Meet Man-de!

Manic-Depressive Ex. Man-de is a cousin to P.E.G., in that she's more than capable of doing every last thing to you that P.E.G. does. It's just that, due to the mercurial nature of her particular mental illness, Man-de isn't as myopic as P.E.G. Look on the bright side: Man-de can at least be nice on those days when she remembers to take her meds.

## 10–19 points = Jerk.

Not her. You, you putz. Truth be told, anyone who's ex scores in this range is entirely healthy and well balanced. There *should* be some fallout from the end of a relationship. It just needs to be a healthy amount. Ask yourself why you didn't work harder to hold on to someone like this. A person who obviously had the mental stability and emotional chutzpah to split up in such a healthy manner is one worth keeping. If you didn't see that, you're the fucking jerk.

## 0–9 points = Mimsy.

. . . Or Buffy, or Emma, or just pick any WASP name, because anyone will do. Christ, if your ex hasn't done any of these things then she's obviously one completely devoid of all emotion, one of those uptight WASPs who get out of the shower to pee.

Well, hopefully this test helped you see some things about your exes and yourself that you can use in future relationships. Next time, though, get a mental health resume on the interview date. And don't let them go on about what an asshole their ex was and how they were wronged and bullshit, whiny, crap, bullshit, crap, crap, crap. If you can, take some time to do some research and find out the circumstances around how they get *into* their relationships. Then see if you can establish a pattern. And if you can, and you find that you're fitting right in? Run the fuck away. If you don't trust me, trust Maya Angelou. I think she said something to this effect: "When they show you who they are—believe them." Honey, you better believe.

Letters

Paul Rudnick is a very strange man. Anyone who has seen his movies and plays, or read his books and articles, knows that Paul should not be allowed to mill about New York City without some sort of watch guard who will stop him from doing harm to himself or others.

This is why it was with some trepidation that I learned of my dubious honor.

## lea's dubious honor

**Paul Rudnick wrote a part specifically for me in his new play, *The Most Fabulous Story Ever Told*.**

It is a lesbian role, which for me is a stretch. I know this may come as a shock to some, but no matter what I have written in this book or may have said in other venues, I am not really a lesbian. The whole thing was a career move.

The name of the character Paul wrote for me is Jane. In order to understand Jane, one must first comprehend the play.

*The Most Fabulous Story Ever Told* is a two-act farce. The first act stands on the premise that God created "Adam and Steve" in the Garden of Eden. I believe Paul meant this as a complicated "fuck you" to Jerry Falwell, as anything involving Jerry and fucking would be complicated.

In the gospel according to Paul Rudnick, God also put Jane and Mabel in the garden. Jane is a big honking diesel butch dyke. Again, a very difficult role for me to portray, as I enjoy rushing home to do girl-type things.

### girl-type things lea enjoys

1. **Arranging flowers**
2. **Cooking and laundry**
3. **Wondering if my jeans make my butt look fat**

Playing Jane allowed me to grow as an actor. In this vehicle I was subtle and insecure, I wept onstage, and I appeared naked. Now I have something in common with Nicole Kidman. Nicole appeared naked in *The Blue Room*. Somehow I feel *The Blue Room* audience enjoyed the view a bit more than the *Most Fabulous* audience.

To The Minetta Lane Theatre,
I vehemently protest against the play *The Most Fabulous Story Ever Told*, which includes a blasphemous reference to the Virgin Mary as a lesbian.

The Holy Mother of God is most pure and sacred. To refer to her as a lesbian, or even to insinuate it, is an unspeakable blasphemy, which I reject with all my soul.

If you continue with this presentation, be sure millions of Catholics will oppose it in one of the largest and loudest peaceful and legal protests ever seen.

Sincerely,

_____

signature

This is the protest postcard circulated by the Catholic Church, which has run out of third-world countries to convert and exploit and now has too much free time.

It seems that Christians get annoyed if anyone toys with the Bible. I find they're a bit much . . . I mean it's not like it's the Bibl . . . er . . . well, or it's holy . . . er, or . . . anything . . . I mean . . . Why waste time with a ridiculous letter-writing campaign to a small off-Broadway* play in the West Village of New York City? Don't you people have an abortion doctor to shoot somewhere?

One day I received a one-page letter dated April 11, 1999. Said letter consisted of one sentence. "I look forward to our meeting." It was signed "Jesus Christ."

I took this to mean he was coming to the show, so I reserved him two tickets for the matinee. Guess what. Jesus stood me up! Can you believe it? I guaranteed those tickets, too. So they took . . . what's $48.50 times two? . . . ninety-seven dollars out of my paycheck, and let's face it, that's a lot of money on an off-Broadway salary. Jesus sucks.

The letters you are about to read are true. The names have been changed to protect the innocent.**

Homosexuals and lesbians CREATED aids by swallowing scman and the sucking of virginias over thousand and thousands of years PART OF YOUR BRAINS IS *SICK.* The Bible does not condone Homosexuality.

Mike Hunt

Obviously the Bible does condone incorrect grammar and spelling.

Not all the Christians are as angered as Mikey. Hugh Jass from Omaha, Nebraska, at least I assume she is from

* And when I say Broadway, I mean Broadway. Stressing the "way," because that's the way Joey Heatherton says it.
** By the innocent, I mean me, from a lawsuit.

Omaha, for so says the postmark on her Mary protest card, tries to help the playwright with this subtle suggestion.

I believe a lesbian Black or Jew or Methodist—would make a better play.

Hugh Jass

Methodist?

This is not acceptable entertainment to Christians.

. . . writes Ms. Ima Nasshole of Woodburg, New Jersey. Actually Ms. Nasshole gave me her return address. I suppose she thought it proper postal etiquette. Perchance we would carry on correspondence regarding Christian entertainment. For my part, I'm glad to have it, for now I can drive by her home, and trade the Mary in the half shell I am certain I will find in her front yard for a darkie jockey holding a lantern. However, I will replace the lantern with this large sign:

### darkie jockey sign

**A Christian lives here.**

**Anyone have a lion**

**we can throw her to?**

I really would like very much to do this to her and her home, except . . . well, even though she does not approve of our little play, and felt she had to let us know, she must have believed it all was too harsh, as below her comment she added this:

Which I take to be the universal symbol for Christian retards.

The beauty of doing controversial work is the countless letters one receives. Even the "thousand and thousands" of protest cards cannot tarnish this beautiful handwritten message:

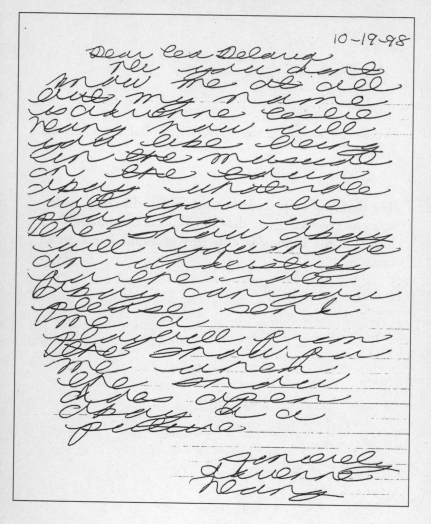

Thanks, I think.

## RULE #8

When they are running

you out of town, dash out

front and pretend you

are leading a parade.

# Detachable Penis

I can't believe they found lube under the bed.

I am a diehard *Law & Order* fan. I watch it on A&E at one o'clock, seven o'clock, and eleven o'clock, knowing full well that seven o'clock is a repeat of one o'clock. On Wednesdays I also get to watch it at ten o'clock. Understand, I have approximately twelve productive awake hours, one third of which are taken up by watching *Law & Order*. This might possibly be why I've never appeared on the series. I'm too busy watching it to audition. That, and the fact that my agent has his thumb up his ass.

I know every assistant D.A.: Claire Kincaid, the second one, the one now, and the black guy. Did I mention Claire Kincaid?

So it was with great anticipation that I prepared myself for the paired *Law & Order/Homicide* episodes that opened the 1999 television season. I got my Orville Redenbacher's Smart Pop popcorn, ninety-eight percent fat free; my Häagen-Dazs frozen yogurt and sorbet bars, totally fat free; and a case of Guinness Stout. I was ready for anything except the discovery of the lube under the murdered woman's bed. It was cherry-flavored Astroglide. That's my brand.

The lube was the first clue in finding that the murder victim was a muff-diving Washington bureaucrat. No, it was not Janet Reno. Lube, on a hit, Emmy-winning, prime-time television show. Lube. And they said Ellen was too gay. Is Annie Sprinkle writing for *Law & Order*?

Can't you picture some farmer in Alabama scratching his balls, eating pigs' snouts and drinking brews, trying to figure out what a lesbian would do with lube? Although I'm quite certain that no one in Alabama watches *Law & Order*. Too many syllables.

In fairness, it's not just Alabamans missing the lesbian-lube connection. Most people do, including lesbians. Have you ever seen a lesbian-made lesbian movie? *Salmonberries, Girl Bar, When Night Is Falling, Claire of the Moon . . .* ZZZZzzzzzzzzzzz. I'm sorry. Did I fall asleep? What we need is the quintessential lesbian-made lesbian movie.

# sister george's personal best children's hour

By
Lillian Bestfoods

INT.

Fade in on steam.

As the steam clears, we see dilapidated lockers, wooden benches, and nuns. We hear the voices of young girls laughing. The camera moves in to reveal it is the shower and locker room of an all-girls Catholic school, St. John the Evangelist.

Sister George, a husky mannish nun, stands over the girls with a clipboard, performing her routine shower inspection.

**SISTER GEORGE**
Mariel.

**MARIEL**
Yes?

**SISTER GEORGE**
You need to towel off better.

**MARIEL**
Why?

**SISTER GEORGE**
Because there's a wet spot there.

Sister George indicates wet spot.

> MARIEL
> It doesn't matter, I'm leaving you for a man.

Fade to black.

INT.

Fade in:

We see a spoonful of stewed tomatoes being plopped on a white Chinet plate on a blue plastic tray.

Camera pans up to reveal Mariel in a Catholic schoolgirl's jumper. Behind her we see other girls eating, throwing food, and laughing. It is the St. John's cafeteria.

Mariel accidentally bumps into Max, a shy young freshman who always wears her baseball cap backward.

> MAX
> Oh my God, I touched another girl. I must be a lesbian.

Max runs out and kills herself.

> MARIEL
> That's okay, I'm leaving you for a man anyway.

Mariel turns and notices Claire, an older, more experienced, attractive senior, watching her. Their eyes meet.

Sister Mary James, a sinewy, husky, somewhat mannish younger nun, steps from the St. John's teachers' lounge carrying her tray. She is cleaning her teeth with her tongue. She notices the glance between the two girls. Sister Mary James crosses to Sister Thomas Aquinas, a pudgy, husky, moderately mannish, in that Merv Griffin kind of way, nun.

> **SISTER MARY JAMES**
> Did you see that?

> **SISTER THOMAS AQUINAS**
> Yes, they're lesbians.

> **SISTER MARY JAMES**
> Oh my God, I've heard the word "lesbian."

She runs off and kills herself.

Fade to black.

INT.

Fade in:

We see stacks of books, a large cross, and a sign that reads: ABSOLUTE QUIET MEANS QUIET ABSOLUTELY. It is the St. John's library.

Mariel and Claire stand across from each other over a study carrel.

> CLAIRE
> Hi.

Mariel smiles.

A nondescript Catholic girl runs into the library screaming.

> NONDESCRIPT CATHOLIC GIRL
> The fox is in the chicken coop again. Oh, and Theresa killed herself.

Sister Richard Marine, an extra-large, husky, extremely mannish nun, crosses with a shotgun on a mission to kill the fox.

> SISTER RICHARD MARINE
> Of course she killed herself. She's a lesbian.

Fade to black.

In the black we hear a clock ticking.

INT.

Mariel asleep in her tiny St. John's cubicle bed.

Cut to:

INT.

Claire asleep in her tiny St. John's cubicle bed.

INT.

Mariel's hands are on her nether regions. However, she has passed out drunk and is unaware.

INT.

Claire's hands are on her breasts. She is dreaming.

DREAM SEQUENCE:

EXT.

Mariel is running in the St. John's soccer field. She is wearing only her St. John's uniform skirt. No shirt. No bra. No panties. She is surrounded by various nuns in varying states of mannishness. She is being chased by the fox and Gina Gershon. As she runs, we get titillating glimpses of her schnooter.

Claire bolts upright, drenched in sweat. Her breasts are heaving. She looks out her window and sees the fox. He appears to be smiling.

Fade to black.

FX: School bell

Kyron: Four years later

INT.

Fade in on steam.

As the steam clears, we see dilapidated lockers, wooden benches, and nuns. We hear the voices of young girls laughing. The camera moves in to reveal it is the St. John's shower and locker room.

Sister George stands over the girls with a clipboard performing her routine shower inspection.

Claire and Mariel are at the back of the line. They are wearing nothing but towels. One of Mariel's supple young breasts is exposed. Claire finally snaps. She grabs Mariel and passionately kisses her, forgetting to use tongue. The coloratura mezzo duet from *Lakmè* plays. Several girls run out of the locker room to kill themselves. Mariel looks at Claire.

**MARIEL**
I'm leaving you for a man.

Cut to:

EXT.

Fade in on steam coming from train smokestack. Sister George is sitting on the train looking out the window as it starts to leave. Claire is running after the train. Sister George yells out the window.

**SISTER GEORGE**
I'm going to New York. Why don't you come
with me.

**CLAIRE**
I will. I will come with you.

Claire is filled with ecstasy as she has finally come to terms with and embraced her lesbianism. She makes a leap for the train, but her hand misses the railing and she is crushed by the wheels.

Fade out as:

The fox laughs.

THE END


No wonder straight people don't know what the lube's for.

Okay. Now we'll start with the dildo conversation.

I have six. All of them black. Most girls want a big black one. Which is why I don't understand the creative use of color as applied to dildos. Pink ones. Blue ones. Marbleized ones. What . . . no metal flake? There are also lavender ones. Although these are usually shaped like an endangered species, with a percentage of their sales going to Greenpeace.

I have six. I used to only have three. Large, extra large, and economy size. Their proper names are: Mr. Big Head, Cinderella's Slipper, and The Terminator. I had to get three more because some girl complained that my cock was too big. Can you do that with your husband?

"Honey, your thing's too big, can we use a smaller one?"

Why should my cock be treated any differently than a man's, when mine is far superior? I have more flexibility. Mine detaches, so as to clean more easily. Are there any men out there who can honestly say they've just boiled their penis?* And let's face it, fellas, how long can you stay hard? My dick is hard right now and it's under my bed in a box.

I've been a butch for a long time. Consequently, I know all there is to know about pros, cons, and obstacles one must face in the use of dildos.

## travel (or, *packing for the girl who packs*)

To avoid embarrassing and time-consuming situations, it is a good idea to keep your sex toys in their own private container. Once, after having boarded a flight to England, I heard my name announced over the plane's PA system. Panicked that there might be some family emergency, I quickly reported to the front of the plane as requested. Once there I was met by airport security.

"Ms. DeLaria, will you please follow me off the plane?"

I protested, concerned that the flight would take off without me. But my fears were assuaged.

"This should only take a moment."

I was led to the security office to find my suitcase sitting on the desk.

"Is this your suitcase?"

I replied in the affirmative.

"Do you have anything electronic in your suitcase?"

I replied in the affirmative again. "I have my cordless microphone in that suitcase."

* This question does not apply to any man who frequents any establishment named The Dungeon.

"I see," said the security guard. "You wouldn't happen to have an alarm clock in there, would you?"

"Why, yes," I proclaimed. "I was in a hurry when I packed and just threw my alarm clock in right next to my cordless microphone . . . and I'll bet that looks just like a bomb, doesn't it?"

The security guard asked me to open my bag and remove the items in question. Worried about the impending take-off, I frantically complied by yanking out the various items. In my haste I caused one carelessly packed double-headed dildo* to fly from the bag and land on the floor directly at the feet of the security guard. Being British, and therefore polite, he immediately bent down to pick it up.

Realizing what it was, he spun on his heels and ran from the room like Elizabeth Berkley in *Showgirls*.

## customs

I knew my trip to Australia was going to be a problem from the moment I applied for my visa. The man taking the information for my application was a homophobic dicknose, horrified that he might have to let me in to his country. After tolerating hours of his condescending tone, I finally snapped. When asked if I had a prison record, I replied, "I didn't know you still needed one to get in."

They have incredibly long lines at customs in Australia. It's just amazing how long the lines are. Take my advice, save yourself the plane fare, queue up in Los Angeles, eventually you'll get to Sydney.

---

* In all honesty, I was not using this particular dildo as a sex toy, it was just a prop in my show. I'm unsure of how a double-headed dildo functions, especially for gay men. "Hey, look! It's Push Me, Pull You."

The reason for this abomination is that customs insists on searching every bag that enters the country.

The agent responsible for my luggage was an attractive Pakistani woman in traditional dress. She spoke with a working-class Australian accent. It took a minute to reconcile the two, so I didn't hear her inquire about my occupation.

"It says here you're an entertainer."

"Yes, I am an entertainer," I replied, but was struck dumb by noticing she had found her way to my sex toys and was holding my handcuffs between her thumb and forefinger.

"Are you a magician?"

"No, honey, I'm just a pervert."

"Okay," she said, as she stamped my passport and allowed me into the country . . . but not before she gave me her phone number.

## take it, don't leave it

I've left vibrators in every hotel in this country.

From now on, when I buy a new vibrator I'm just going to have it stamped COURTESY OF THE GIDEONS.

I was halfway to the airport before I realized that I had left every sex toy I owned at the Vancouver Sheraton.

"Oh my God, I've castrated myself!"

I don't usually travel with every sex toy I own. There are far too many.

### every sex toy lea owns

#### 1. Mr. Big Head

#### 2. Cinderella's Slipper

3. The Terminator

4. Mr. Peepers

5. Two tiny unnamed penises that I bought for the stupid bitch in Portland, Oregon, who dumped me right after I spent $150 on two tiny penises.

6. A strap

7. Two bottles of lube (just in case)

8. Leather gloves

9. A paddle

10. Handcuffs

11. Silk ties

12. Leather ties

13. Fur-lined leg cuffs

14. Angelina Jolie

I brought every sex toy I owned because I was touring Canada and I find Canadian women extremely sexy. And easy.

"Turn around. Turn around! Turn around!! Turn around!!!" I screamed at the limo driver, who shot me a look of confusion.

"Gottagobackgottagobackgottagoback!"

I jumped out of the car the second he pulled up in front of the hotel, and raced to the elevator, leaving a trail of bruised, apologetic Canadians in my wake. I heard the last one say, "I'm sorry," just as the elevator closed on his face.

I sprinted down the hall to my room and rounded the

corner to find I was too late. There she stood in the doorway, wrapping the cord around her vacuum cleaner, having just finished readying my room for the next business traveler. My maid.

My maid was a ninety-year-old Asian woman. How do you ask a ninety-year-old Asian woman if she found your ten-inch rubber cock?

"Excuse me . . . Did you find . . . anything . . . in my room?"

The ninety-year-old Asian woman said, "Oh, you mean your dildos? Here."

Then she handed me every sex toy I owned in a "Thank you for staying at the Sheraton—We appreciate your patronage!" plastic bag.

I ran out so fast, I forgot to tip her. But I'll never forget her. Thank you, ninety-year-old Asian woman. You saved my life.

## RULE #9

If someone makes a point of
saying they are not doing
something, they are.

### examples of saying they are not doing something they are

1. I'm not saying this to hurt you, but...

2. I'm not angry, but...

3. I'm not leaving you for someone else, but...

# The Butch
## and
## the Bichick

## today

Today I woke up with a bisexual girl . . . again. One might say I woke up on the wrong side of the bed, except bisexuals have no wrong side of the bed.

Experience teaches me bichicks have three characteristics in common.

### common bichick characteristics

1. They are fascinated by me.

2. They always leave me for a man.

3. In between they pick my pocket.

This particular bichick has *issues*. Note: I italicize "issues" in the preceding sentence in order to clarify her pointedness, rather than as a means of expressing my sarcasm that I assume you assumed, as this one is REALLY ALL ABOUT her "issues." Issues. Issues. Issues. Everybody and their issues. "Don't yell at me, I have issues. My mother always yelled at me before she locked me in the closet. This is an issue." Hey, Sybil! If your mother locked you in the closet, it is a travesty. It is a painful memory. It is a classic case of blatant child abuse. What it is *not* is an "issue." An issue is when you are waiting in line to use the bathroom at an elegantly swank party in the Upper Sixties; just as you notice the plush and full design of the white shag carpet, you sneeze and blow your tampon out one-quarter inch.

The word "issue" is enjoying much too large a share of the Nielsens lately. Let's refer to them as "tissues." You pull one out and another pops up.

### this bichick's tissues

1. Parents

2. Privacy

Let's explore these one at a time, shall we? Mmmn?*

## bichick tissue number one

### Parents

By parents, she actually means Mom, or, as she calls her, "Mommy." The more observant reader has just reflexed a sharp intake of breath upon seeing the word "Mommy." This reader is remembering my announced proclivity for young women and by now is uncomfortably wondering how old this bichick is. Allow me to lay your fears to rest. She can order drinks in a bar. She owns a fake I.D.

Bichick's mom is of Germanic decent, having grown up in Düsseldorf during the war. That must make the Bichick Mum extremely *emotionally present*.**

On the whole, I don't find Germans to be very emotional. Once, while traveling in Bavaria, I developed a cough. I searched endlessly through countless *drogeriemarkt* in vain, desperately seeking a cough suppressant. Then suddenly, I realized, "They don't sell cough sup-

---

* Bichick, if you are reading this, it is my sincerest hope you have already left me for a man.

** Now, this phrase is italicized to express sarcasm.

pressants in Germany. Suppressants are unnecessary. If a German does not wish to cough, he won't."

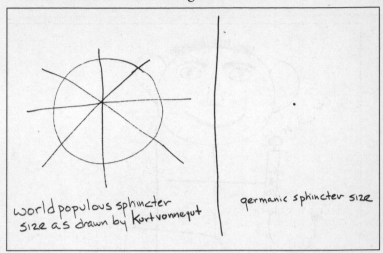

world populous sphincter size as drawn by Kurt vonnegut

germanic sphincter size

I do love Germans; they're such victims of their own behavior.

This notion isn't born out of a vacuum. I had a previous experience with a Germanic mother-in-law, while dating one of my first teenage sweethearts. (I am, by way of explanation, referring to myself as the teenager.) The Kleine Deutsche Mädchen decided we had to tell the Mutti.

"*Mutti, wo bist du?*" the Deutsche Mädchen queries as I nervously glance about the Joan-Crawford–clean, everythinghasaplace spartan house I am visiting for the first time.

I think, *She's most probably in the kitchen seeing if she can stick a pin up her ass.*

"I'm in the kitchen," her mother replies.

We enter the pristine kitchen to discover Mutti on her hands and knees, busily involved in some project or other. Making lamp shades, no doubt.

## me stepping across the line
**(Please note the satanic grin.)**

"Mutti," Deutsche Mädchen says, "I want you to meet Lea. She's my girlfriend. I'm a lesbian."

I brace myself for the hurricane that I expect, having recently come out to my own parents. Mama Mia and Papa Mia handled it in typical Guinea Wop Dago greaseball fashion. There was the screaming, there was the yelling. There was the dinette sailing through the kitchen window. Then they forgot and we had to repeat the whole thing again.

### mia
Ma. Why are you introducing me to a Vito.
I don't want to know a "Vito."

**<u>papa mia</u>**
He's a nice boy.

**<u>mia</u>**
*I'm* a nice boy. I'm gaygaygaygaygaygayGAY. Don't you remember the dinette on the back lawn?

**<u>papa mia</u>**
Wasn't that from a tornado?

**<u>mia</u>**
We don't live in a trailer park. You threw it out the window because I'm gay.

**<u>mama mia</u>**
Don't say that.

**<u>mia</u>**
Gay. Gay fruit fairy lesbian.

**<u>mama mia and papa mia</u> (unison)**
Oh! (beat) Lesbian's an ugly word.

**<u>mia</u>**
Dyke, then.

**<u>mama mia and papa mia</u> (unison)**
Oh!

**<u>papa mia</u>**
It's justa phase.

**<u>mia</u>**
Phase? I watch *Cagney & Lacey* reruns. I have every album Laura Nyro ever made. Look at my feet—have you ever seen a more comfortable pair of shoes?

**papa mia**
Well.

**mia**
I have a life-size poster of Martina Navratilova
hanging over my bed.

**papa mia**
Basta. Basta. Okay. Enough. I get it. We had girls
like you in the army.

**mia**
Probably every one of them. Gay.

**papa mia**
Enough.
(There is a beat.)

**mama mia**
So maybe tomorrow Vito could stop by.
You two could talk.

After Deutsche Mädchen's blunt pronouncement, Mutti
set aside what appeared to be a scalpel she'd been using to
shape the shade. Slowly she turned toward us. She spoke
calmly without moving her face, or even the hair on her
face.

"It makes me sick. Girls doing all zat, zat sucking and
licking and poking vit zier fingers."

I blinked, and thought, *Well, Mrs. Mengele, just what
other little ideas have popped into your head as you leaf
through your* Redbook *magazine?*

The Bichick Mum has issues* with the gay thing due to
previous experience—one of the Bichick siblings, the

* AAARGHH!!

Bichick Brother, to be exact, came out to the Bichick Mum. He told her he was "gay as a box of birdseed," or "friend of Dorothy," or some such nonsense.

Those sorts of tired old queen expressions are horribly dated. We need a new generation of nancy-boy-type identification. The kind that will be suitable for the new millennium. May I suggest some of these?

### nancy-boy-type identifications*

1. He has an ear for music.

2. Oh, him? He's a figure skater.

3. He speaks Norwegian. With an accent.

So the Bichick Brother gathers the Bichick Family into the Bichick Living Room and makes the big pronouncement.

"I speak Norwegian," says he.

"With an accent?" the mortified Bichick Mum gasps.

"With an accent," the Bichick Brother replies, while raising an eyebrow and rolling his eyes.

The Bichick Family begins to cry. I should point out that this is extremely difficult for Germans, who mostly import their tears from Portugal, Spain, or sometimes even Turkey when there is no war and the Turks have a surplus.

So without help from customs, the entire Bichick Family burst into histrionics—everyone, that is, except the Bichick Brother. He crows. He is Peter Pan. He jumps about, released from the shackles of his dirty little secret. In front of his distraught family he has the audacity to be happy.

* When uttering these, one should raise an eyebrow and roll the eyes during "ear for music," "figure skater," and "with an accent."

Then he scurries off to shop, as he has tickets for Liza and nothing to wear.

## bichick tissue number two

### privacy

### definition of privacy
### (taken from *The Oxford English Dictionary*)

**The state or condition of being withdrawn from the society of others or from public attention; freedom from the disturbance or intrusion; seclusion.**

### definition of privacy
### (taken from the bichick)

**No displays of intimacy.**

Once upon a time, long long ago, in a land far away, I found myself ensconced in a monogamous relationship. It seems a part of my life lived in a different yet dreamlike existence, as I have always found monogamy to make very pretty chifforobes, though my preference is for chestnut or oak. Interviewers quite often ask, "Lea, what is it you look for in a woman?"

"A vagina" is my usual response.

Alas, this was apparently not always so, because once upon a time, long long ago, in a land far away, at the center of a dreamlike existence . . . I . . . thought . . . I . . . was . . . in love!

## the object of my affection

The Object of My Affection was a gorgeous woman. Gorgeous only to those into the stunning type. I usually find myself attached to beautiful women. The reason for this is quite simple. I am shallow. The Object of My Affection was half Persian, half French, raised in England. She spoke five different languages and knew how to say, "Buy me this," in all of them.

When I would shout epithets, such as "Eat my ass, you fucking cunt," she, being British, would calmly pat my thigh and say, "Don't be tacky, dahling." It was like dating a Noël Coward play.

The Object of My Affection, besides being a pillow princess—i.e., "I'll lie here and you worship me"—was even more terrified of intimacy than I. To be more terrified of intimacy than I is a daunting task, especially when considering the DeLaria intimacy fact sheet.

### delaria intimacy fact sheet

1. In my entire adult life I have never had a serious relationship with someone residing in the same city as me.

   a. In fact, I find a continent between us provides me with enough "space."

   b. The Object of My Affection lived in London. I lived in Los Angeles . . . so a continent *and* an ocean gave me a little breathing room.

2. Sprint often accompanies my phone bill with thank-you notes and long-stemmed roses. You know, Sprint, I think free access to 550 numbers would be more fitting.

1–900–PEEE, "the extra E is for extra Pee." Extra pee? Who has extra pee? I've always peed just enough, thank you. What New Yorker has not found him- or herself staring hypnotized, almost transfixed, at Robin Byrd banging who knows whose box. "Channel 35 . . . I want my S/MTV!" I believe my favorite sexfomercial shows a famous female porn star spanking some bruised-bottomed bottom while evilly growling, "Say it. Say it." The bruised-bottomed bottom wriggles and groans in an attempt at the portrayal of masochistic ecstasy, which in actuality sounds more like the Elizabeth Taylor sick-horse-in-the-barn wails from *National Velvet*. Just when you are quite certain it can't get any funnier than this, at just that point, you notice the famous porn star is *brutally* spanking her bruised-bottomed bottom with a ninety-nine-cent flyswatter. A *flyswatter*. Where exactly does one find a flyswatter in Pandora's Box? Aisle one . . . penis enlargers, leather masks, slings, and flyswatters. I suppose aisle two has the electric toys such as vibrators and bug lights. It's hard for me to admit that my mother has been clearing away insects at family functions using a sex toy. Personally, if I was that famous porn star I would not be nastily demanding my bruised-bottomed bottom to "Say it. Say it" while spanking her with a *swatter*. Instead I'd be more inclined toward "Bad fly!" Whack. "Bad fly!" Whack. "Who's your larva!?!" Whack.

One day we—the Object of My Affection and I—found ourselves embroiled in a heated discussion. Such was the nature of our relationship. Such is the nature of any relationship between an American and a Brit, or a Brit and any other nationality, for that matter.

The English have a tendency toward the superiority complex, an odd tendency when one considers the centerpiece of their morning meal, Marmite. For those who are unaware, Marmite is a substance spread on toast and consumed with a nice "cupper." As far as science has been able to determine, the molecular structure of Marmite is primarily heavily salted, squashed cold pooh.

Our discussion/argument reached the pinnacle when I released like a steam valve my fears and deep insecurities, my desires regarding us and our future . . . the "Commitment Conversation." After a moment, the Object of My Affection spoke. "I just don't feel like we have any intimacy." What? There I sat, tears in my eyes, having poured my soul into a salad bowl, where I tossed it with wooden tongs and served it up dressed in fresh balsamic. SHE DOESN'T BELIEVE WE HAVE INTIMACY!?!

The Object of My Affection continued, "Actually, I'm not even sure I know what intimacy is."

There was a time in my life when I had no idea what an orgasm was, until I experienced one. Then I knew.

The Bichick Privacy Tissue can be subdivided into three categories.

### bichick privacy tissue subdivision

a. **No displays of intimacy in public**

b. **No displays of intimacy at her place of employment**

c. **No displays of intimacy at her home**

Suffice it to say we spend a lot of time at my place. Okay, no displays of intimacy. In order to comply, one must first comprehend "intimacy." Like my old Object of Affection, I am uncertain of exactly what the Bichick means by "intimacy." I personally cannot tolerate grown people amorously kissing in public, although I do thoroughly enjoy a rousing round of sex in inappropriate places.

I decide to test the question. I reach out to grasp the Bichick hand. Bichick quickly pulls away.

"We are in public," comes the Bichick hiss.

Indeed we are. We are in Union Square on Farmers Market Day. All the booths abound. It is an amazing spectacle when one considers the previous state of Union Square. There was a time when the only purchases made here were needles and poontang. Now it is a sea of white people, all of them milling about their flowers and breads and tomatoes on the vine. None of them really has time to notice the Butch and the Bichick.

I put my hands in my pockets, a gesture I have perfected over a course of years. This gesture helps me avoid strangling bichicks.

"It's hardly public," I say, being butch.

"It's Union Square," comes the Bichick response, her being femme and therefore manipulative.

"Union Square," I continue, "might as well be Washington Square, and Washington Square is the veritable clitoris of the West Village. The West Village is the fucking center of Queerdom. And I can't hold your fucking hand because it's an intimate public display?"

The Bichick glances nervously around. "Do you have to say 'clitoris' so loudly?"

## bichick overload

I retreat to a state of inordinate butchness. To be more plain . . . I pout.

The Bichick pats my back, which I assume is not a display of intimacy.

"Look. I just don't wish to be obvious in public."

As she speaks, the Bichick gesticulates the universal sign for quotation marks around the word "obvious." It is a hand motion the Bichick makes with great frequency, like some strange form of Tourette's syndrome, to over-emphasize her emphasis.

Then we notice "Her."

## her

"Her" is a fortyish trying to look thirtyish Hispanic woman. You have to love the Puerto Rican/Mexican/South and Central Americans; they are the only people who can wear red, turquoise, silver, and gold at the same time.

"Her" is attired in a very tight red dress with turquoise trim. Since her youth attempt is in full swing, her dress is much too small and tight for "Her," making "Her" appear to be a walking spandex sausage.

"Her" feet are the main attraction. "Her" feet are squeezed into what appears to be silver spray-painted platform pumps.

*There is a Tin Man quality to those shoes,* I think, and as I think it the Bichick begins to skip behind "Her."

"Follow the yellow brick road," the Bichick sings, as she skips. "Follow the yellow brick road."

Yet holding hands is too much of a public display.

## tonight

Tonight I fell asleep with a bisexual girl . . . again.

We have just made very sweet love. She came in my mouth with my fingers inside of her. Then she cried in my arms until she fell into slumber. I spoon myself around her and take in her fragrance.

I am falling in love with the Bichick . . . heaven help me.

## RULE #10

Learn all the rules . . .

then break them.

# BIBLIOGRAPHY

1. *The Diary of Anne Frank*, by Anne Frank
2. *Moby Dick*, by Jeff Stryker
3. *Heather Has Three Mommies, Now Try to Explain That to Your Kid*, by Susie "Not So" Bright
4. *The Complete Diary of Anne Frank*, by Anne Frank
5. *To Sir, with Love*, by Marcie
6. *The Unabridged Diary of Anne Frank*, by Anne Frank
7. *A Christian's Guide to the Millennium Bug*, by Jerry Falwell
8. *How to Bug a Christian*, by Lea DeLaria
9. *The Completely Unabridged Diary of Anne Frank*, by Anne Frank
10. *Stop Making These Movies*, by Jane Austen
11. *Black Like Me*, by Michael Jackson
12. *I Can't Do Anything But Come Out*, by Chastity Bono
13. *Silence of the Gams*, by Jodie Foster
14. *The Missionary Position*, by Mother Teresa
15. *The "We Found These Pages in the Ladies' Room at the Reichsmuseum" Diary of Anne Frank*, by Anne Frank
16. *Chicken Soup for the Sphincter*, by Richard Simmons
17. *As I Lay Dying*, by the World Economy
18. *The Diary of Barney Frank*, by Ani DiFranco

# ABOUT THE AUTHOR

Lea DeLaria has been a professional lesbian since the early 1980s. Before that time Lea mostly freelanced while working days as a heterosexual. If Lea were a tree she'd be the palm tree in Angelina Jolie's bedroom.